AF788999

Information Technology Law in South Africa

Information Technology Law in South Africa

Daniel van der Merwe

This book was originally published as a monograph in the International Encyclopaedia of Laws/Privacy and Technology Law.

Founding Editor: Roger Blanpain
General Editor: Frank Hendrickx
Volume Editors: Jos Dumortier, Pieter Gryffroy, Ruben Roex & Yung Shin Van Der Sype

Wolters Kluwer

Published by:
Kluwer Law International B.V.
PO Box 316
2400 AH Alphen aan den Rijn
The Netherlands
E-mail: lrs-sales@wolterskluwer.com
Website: www.wolterskluwer.com/en/solutions/kluwerlawinternational

Sold and distributed by:
Wolters Kluwer Legal & Regulatory U.S.
920 Links Avenue
Landisville, PA 17538
United States of America
E-mail: customer.service@wolterskluwer.com

ISBN 978-94-035-2286-9

e-Book: ISBN 978-94-035-2516-7
web-PDF: ISBN 978-94-035-2526-6

The Author

Daniel (Dana) van der Merwe was born in Oudtshoorn, South Africa on 31 December 1947. He studied at the University of Port Elizabeth, South Africa (now Nelson Mandela University) (B-Juris 1968) and the University of South Africa (LLB 1972, LLD 1980). He also obtained a certificate in Electronic Law from the University of Cape Town in May 2002. Van der Merwe has published widely. Two of his works are *Sentencing* (Juta 1980) and *Computers and the Law* (Juta 1986 and 2000). The first edition of the latter book was the first of its kind for Africa and one of the earliest expositions of this area of law in the world. His latest works on this topic are *Information and Communications Technology (ICT) Law* (LexisNexis 2008, a second edition in 2016 and a third in 2022). He has also published many articles in refereed journals, locally and internationally, in the latter part of his career, mostly in the area of ICT law. He has drafted parts on computer crime and on the law of evidence of South Africa's Electronic Communications and Transactions Act 25 of 2002, the first of its nature on the African continent. His present research interests are in eXtensible Markup Language (XML) and eXtensible Business Reporting Language (XBRL) and the influence which these data formats may exercise on advanced electronic signatures as well as on mobile and electronic commerce in general. He is also interested in new ways in which ICT may be used to make teaching at the tertiary level more effective, particularly by making use of cellular technology.

The Author

Table of Contents

List of Abbreviations

5G	Fifth Generation (of cellular technology)
ADR	Alternative Dispute Resolution
AFSA	Arbitration Federation of South Africa
AIPO	African Intellectual Property Organization
AITSA	Association for Information Technology of South Africa
ANC	African National Congress
ARIPO	African Regional Intellectual Property Organization
ANSAC	American Natural Soda Ash Corporation
BBBEEAC	Broad-Based Black Economic Empowerment Advisory Council
BBC	Black Business Council
B2B	Business-to-Business
B2C	Business-to-Consumer
BRICS	Brazil, Russia, India, China and South Africa
CAC	Competition Appeal Court
CCTV	Closed-Circuit Television
CD-ROM	Compact Disk, Read-Only Memory
CE	Council of Europe
CRAM	Computer Random Access Memory
CSSA	Computer Society of South Africa
CONTU	Committee on New Technical Uses of Copyrighted Works
DAT	Digital Audio Tape
DOC	Department of Communications
DVD	Digital Video Disk
EC	Electronic Communications
ECT	Electronic Communications and Transactions (Act)

List of Abbreviations

EDI	Electronic Data Interchange
EFT	Electronic Funds Transfer
FAST	Federation Against Software Theft
FBI	Federal Bureau of Investigation
FTC	Federal Trade Commission
GATT	General Agreement on Tariffs and Trade (GG Government Gazette)
GEAR	Growth, Employment and Redistribution
GG	Government Gazette
HDPE	High Density Polyethelene Pipes
HTML	Hypertext Markup Language
HTTP	Hypertext Transfer Protocol
IBA	Independent Broadcasting Authority
ICASA	Independent Communications Authority of South Africa
ICP	International Civil Procedure
ICT	Information and Communications Technology
ICs	Integrated Circuits
IFLA	International Federation of Librarians and Archivists
IJS	Integrated Justice System
IOT	Internet of Things
ISPA	Internet Service Providers' Association
ISO	International Standards Organization
IT	Information Technology
JCPS	Justice, Crime Prevention and Security Cluster'
JOC	Judgments on Copyright
LAN	Local Area Network
LLM	Master of Laws
LTE	Long Term Evolution
MIDI	Musical Instrument Digital Interface
OSP	Online Service Provider
Para(s)	Paragraph(s)
PAIA	Protection of Access to Information Act
PIL	Private International Law
PKI	Public Key Infrastructure
PROATIA	Promotion of Access to Information (Act)
POPI	Protection of Personal Information
POTS	Plain Old Telephone System
RAM	Random Access Memory

ROICAPOCRIA (RIC for short)	Regulation of Interception of Communications and Provision of Communication-Related Information Act
RSA	Rivest-Shamir-Adleman
SAA	South African Airways
SAB	South African Breweries
SABS	South African Bureau for Standards
SACC	*South African Journal of Criminal Law and Criminology*
SACR	South African Criminal Law Reports
SAIIPL	South African Institute of Intellectual Property Lay
SITA	State Information Technology Agency
SALC	South African Law Commission
SAPS	South African Police Service
SAPO	South African Post Office
SASOL	South African Synthetic Oils
SATRA	South African Telecommunications Regulatory Authority
SGML	Standard Generalized Markup Language
SKYPE	Sky Peer to Peer
SMEs	Small and Medium Enterprises
SNO	Second National Operator
SOEs	State-owned Enterprises
TRIPS	Trade-Related Aspects of Intellectual Property Rights
TSPs	Telecommunication Service Providers
UCC	Uniform Commercial Code
UK	United Kingdom
US	United States
UNCITRAL	United Nations Commission on International Trade Law
VAT	Value Added Tax
VOIP	Voice Over Internet Protocol
WCT	WIPO Copyright Treaty
WIPO	World Intellectual Property Organization
WST	Warplas Share Trust
WTO	World Trade Organization
XBRL	eXtensible Business Reporting Language
XML	eXtensible Markup Language

List of Abbreviations

ZAR	South African Rand

General Introduction

Chapter 1. General Background of the Country

§1. Geography and History

1. Present-day South Africa has come about as the result of a variety of changes. It has been home to the San tribes for many centuries. In 1652 it became a Dutch colony, was annexed as a British colony from the beginning of the nineteenth century and formed the Union of South Africa in 1910 from the Cape Colony, Natal, and the former Boer (or Dutch-speaking) republics of Transvaal and the Orange Free State. The Union did not give voting rights to the many citizens of Black, Indian or Coloured heritage.

2. In 1961, it became the Republic of South Africa and left the British Commonwealth, mainly as a result of criticism of its apartheid (racist) policies. In 1995, an election was held based on universal franchise for the first time, and Nelson Mandela became president of a multiracial South Africa. The country is situated on the southern tip of the continent of Africa. Because of its latitude and the fact that most of the interior lies high above sea level, South Africa possesses a generally cooler and more temperate climate than the rest of Africa. Parts of the country are subject to extended periods of drought and, therefore, remain sparsely populated.

3. Traditionally, the economy remained dependent on farming and mining (South Africa is blessed with great mineral wealth), but during the twentieth century, the country has become industrialized, including several unique projects such as the South African Synthetic Oils (SASOL) project which extracts oil from coal. South Africa has taken to Information and Communications Technology (ICT) enthusiastically and a number of Information Technology (IT) firms, such as Datatec are listed on the stock exchange. Internet service providers (ISPs) such as M-Web deliver services which are equal to any in the rest of the world. South African Internet Service Providers have organized themselves into ISPA or the Internet Service Providers' Association.

§2. HISTORICAL BACKGROUND TO THE LEGAL SYSTEM

I. Roman-Dutch Common Law

4. Upon the second (and final) conquest of the Cape Colony by the British in 1806, the legal system introduced by the prior Dutch colonists remained in force. This was in line with the British case of *Campbell v. Hall*,[1] which determined that any local legal system of a new British colony would remain in place until specifically repealed. This led to the interesting result that the substantive law of the Cape Colony remained substantially (no pun intended) Roman-Dutch, whereas the adjective or formal law became transformed into English law. The latter change was necessary in order that the new British magistrates and judges were able to understand and enforce the rules of evidence as well as criminal and civil procedure. This situation was later extended to Natal, the Orange Free State, and the Transvaal, thus comprising the four[2] different provinces of the later Union of South Africa.

5. Other areas that were transformed into British law by means of subject-specific legislation were company law as well as the law of taxation, insolvency, intellectual property, and negotiable instruments.

II. South African Law

6. It is of the utmost importance to note that South African law has never been subject to general codification, as has happened to most European systems. Thus, South Africa is unique in being a civil-law country (for at least 50% of its substantive law), whose law (including private as well as public law) is uncodified but with a (British-based) statutory system for many areas of commerce, for instance, company and insurance law. This development includes civil and criminal procedures, including the law of evidence. The latter systems are characterized by the accusatorial nature of their criminal process. Coming from this background, the law of evidence remains as important in the legal panoply as it would in common-law countries such as the United Kingdom (UK) and the United States (US). Nonetheless, the jury system was abolished during the middle of the twentieth century in South Africa, the result (some say) of the failure to get convictions by jury of illicit diamond buying charges in the Kimberley district.

7. That left the country with complicated rules concerning the admissibility of evidence which are typical of jury trials, even though the jury has disappeared. Only evidence that has survived scrutiny in terms of these rules of admissibility, amplified since 1994 by strong constitutional protection of suspected, arrested, and accused persons, can be evaluated for weight in the relevant proceedings. Strictly

1. (1774) 1 Cowper 204, 98 ER 1045.
2. The new South Africa (since 1994) now has nine provinces, namely Gauteng, North-West Province, Mpumalanga, Limpopo, Northern Cape, Eastern Cape, Western Cape, Kwazulu-Natal, and the Free State.

speaking, the court should not be hamstrung by the present complex of complicated rules of admissibility, because South Africa no longer has the problem of a decision-making body consisting of lay jurors. A court may sometimes sit with assessors, but the assessors are specifically chosen for their expertise – sometimes in the area of constitutional protection arising from the South African constitution adopted by a government elected by general franchise (for the first time) in 1995. In terms of the test laid down by Packer in his work, *The Limits of the Criminal Sanction*,[3] South Africa has moved from a 'crime control' model to a 'due process' model. This imposes a strict regime on investigating authorities, which is not helped by the fact that intricate permutations between hardware and software may have to be investigated.

8. There have been a number of South African court cases in which technical (and digital) data, either from computers or cell phones, have been tendered to the court in evidence. In this instance, one thinks of the Gatiep Pietersen murder trial,[4] the *Judge Motata* case[5] of alleged drunken driving and the *Boeremag* case.[6] These will be discussed in the section on evidence below (*see* below Part III Online Transactions and in particular Chapter 2 Electronic Signatures and Chapter 3 Law of Evidence in the Digital Environment).

3. 1968.
4. 'Najwa escapes life at <http://news.iafrica.com> of 11 Feb. 2009 and referring to the conviction of Najwa Petersen on the murder of her entertainer-musician husband.
5. *S v. Nikola John Motata* (Jhb Regional Court case 63/968/07), which was probably the longest-running drunken driving case in South African legal history.
6. *S v. Du Toit and Others* (unreported TPD case CC 91/2003). This was definitely the longest-running treason trial in South African legal history and indicated how SA judges make heavy weather of ICT-related cases.

9. Traditionally, the South African Post Office was in charge not only for delivering surface mail but also for the provision of the plain old telephone system (POTS) over the whole of South Africa. This was no mean task, given the sparsely populated nature of a great part of South Africa, especially the dry interior of the western part of the country. Thus, every small town had its general post office, which sold postage stamps, accepted payments on telephone accounts and acted as a savings bank, etc. for the farming community. Telegraph and telephone lines were often the only landmarks in the featureless veldt.

10. During the latter part of the twentieth century, the postal service split into two independent parts, namely the traditional South African Post Office (SAPO) (which continued to handle the traditional postal services) and Telkom, which received a virtual monopoly on telecommunications services from the South African government. As time went on and telecommunications became a worldwide business, the Telkom monopoly became more and more controversial.[7] After years of promises, the then South African Minister of Communications, Ivy Matsepi-Casaburri, finally approved and announced a Second National Operator (SNO) in 2004. This body entered the arena as 'Neotel' and provided telecommunications services as the only competition for Telkom. In October 2016, a firm known as 'Liquid Intelligent Technologies' obtained unconditional approval from ICASA to acquire Neotel. By transforming itself as a cellular service provider Telkom still seems to be doing reasonably well financially, but SAPO has recently struggled to cover its weekly salary bill – perhaps an institution for which the need has expired? At the time of writing, it seems incapable of delivering hard copies of books or magazines (such as *TIME*), as the present author has discovered to his own cost. The only alternative seems to be the downloading of electronic versions of such works.

11. The Internet itself had its birth in South Africa in the academic sector, when Rhodes University in Grahamstown (now Makhanda) established the first sustainable e-mail link with a private home in Portland, Oregon, US, a link which was later connected to the Internet.[8] At the same time, the state-funded Foundation for Research and Development started a network among South African universities called Uninet. The Voice over Internet Protocol was announced by (the then) Telecommunications Minister Matsepi-Casaburri for South Africa in September 2002. A heartening development has been the success of a firm called Sky Peer to Peer (SKYPE) in providing Voice over Internet Protocol (VOIP) services.[9] Other flavours of SKYPE have been developed in various countries, such as British Telecom, Vonage from the US, and Vanadoo of France.[10] Skype has since been taken over by Microsoft – a symbol of its success. South Africa has produced firms such as Broadband Talk (the latter service provided by M-Web, one of the first ordinary

7. Spawning a number of protest websites, one of which was entitled 'Hellkom'.
8. Lawrie, as quoted in *Cyberlaw@SA*, 1st ed. (Van Schaiks, 2000).
9. Van der Merwe et al., *ICT Law*, 3d ed. (LexisNexis Durban, 2022): 17.
10. *Ibid.*

ISPs in Southern Africa.).[11] Online teaching has been gaining hand-over-fist during the two-year long COVID-19 pandemic. Programs such as 'Zoom' and Microsoft's 'Teams' are handy in this regard, provided that the classes are not too large. The latest development has been a move to fibre which promises a great increase in transmission speed and this medium has, therefore, been adopted by many service providers. Changes in the regulatory structure to accommodate some of the other recent developments will be discussed below.[12]

11. *Ibid.*
12. *See* Ch. 3 *infra* for private sector and Ch. 5 *infra* for public sector developments.

Chapter 3. The Information and Communications Technology Market

12. In the words of Professor Michael Rappa,[13] 'business models are perhaps the most discussed and least understood aspect of the Web'. As with the gold rushes of the nineteenth century, more participants end up bankrupt than the lucky (or skilful?) ones who make their fortune on the Web. Unfortunately, this is still all too true for the black population of South Africa, despite the efforts of the Black Business Council (BBC) in establishing a 'black bank' and asserting influence in South Africa's Broad-Based Black Economic Empowerment Advisory Council (BBBEEAC). Of course, the present COVID-19 pandemic has not been kind to start-up enterprises.

South Africa has had a few Internet success stories to date. One of these was the South African equivalent of amazon.com, called Kalahari.Net. This site used to be South Africa's largest 'e-tailing'[14] company has now been taken over by an overseas firm called (somewhat rudely) 'Takealot', still selling books, software, souvenirs, and other odds and ends.[15] Another example is the South African portal at M-Web,[16] which offers a large virtual shopping mall consisting of many smaller malls specializing in specific product categories, such as music, books, sport, etc.

13. Another very successful spin-off of the Internet has been the phenomenon known as 'blogging'. A formal definition could be as follows:

> A blog (a truncation of the term 'Web log') is a Web site, is a discussion or informational site published on the World Wide Web consisting of discrete entries ('posts') typically displayed in reverse chronological order. such as graphics or video. Entries are commonly displayed in reverse-chronological order (the most recent post appears first).

14. In a commentary on this phenomenon entitled 'Blogging as a fad is over, serious blogging arrives', Arthur Goldstuck describes how blogging has developed in South Africa from a lightweight fad to an apparent tipping point for social media and social networking in South Africa.[17]

---

13. In an article entitled 'Business Models on the Web' (2000) available at <www.ecommerce. ncsu.edu /business-models.html>
14. 'E-tailing' may be defined as 'Business-to-consumer e-commerce'.
15. *See* <www.takealot.com>.
16. To be found at <www.mweb.co.za>.
17. At <www.techleader.com/amablogoblogo/2008/03/26. 'Who shakes & shapes the blogging field'.

Chapter 4. e-Commerce: Facts and Figures

§1. Development of Internet-Based e-Commerce

15. From the latter part of the 1980s, South African access to international telecommunications networks was restricted because of universal disapproval of the political situation in South Africa. However, towards the end of the twentieth century, South Africa had developed into one of the top-twenty connected countries in the world, probably because apartheid had ended, and Nelson Mandela was elected as president in the first elections with universal suffrage in 1994. At that time, South Africa had more than eighty ISPs and more than a million Internet users. By the end of 2001, this had grown to 2.89 million South African Internet users.[18] However, this means that South Africa still has only one Internet connection for every 342 people, thus lagging far behind countries such as Hong Kong, Singapore, and Taiwan.

16. As far as 2021 is concerned, the following figures make clear the degree of Internet penetration within South Africa:[19] As of January 2021, South Africa had 38.3 million active Internet users, 36.13 million active mobile Internet users, 25 million active social media users and 24.63 million active mobile social media users.

17. In part of the latest developments, as described by Arthur Goldstuck,[20] he indicates how SA enterprises have taken a backward step during the first year of the COVID-19 pandemic. This disappointing result came about despite expectations that working remotely or from home (an 'electronic cottage') would prevent such a slowdown. This also affected industries such as commercial property providers as well as providers of the necessary infrastructure at the workplace.

18. In recent years Internet commerce (e-commerce) has increased exponentially, especially because it has now grown very popular by means of cell phones. Goldberg indicates how SA enterprises in the area of cell phones (mobile or m-commerce) have taken a backward step as a result of COVID. However, in South Africa, many black users who have traditionally never had access to computers are now able to buy and sell electronically by means of the (more affordable) mobile technology. Mobile commerce in South Africa has been called 'an established and growing phenomenon.'[21]

§2. Types of e-Commerce

19. In the traditional business-to-business (B2B) type of e-commerce, most businesses still avail themselves of the tried and trusted electronic data interchange

18. Goldstuck, as quoted in *Managing E-Commerce* (2004) Juta at 121.
19. 'Digital population in South Africa as of January 2021'.
20. In a note entitled 'Remote working needs digital sauce'. .
21. Van der Merwe et al., *ICT Law*, 3rd ed. (2022): 162 n3.

(EDI). Even before this, South Africa was an early adopter of microfilm and actually started an organization called the Association for Information Technology of South Africa (AITSA). With the decline in the use of this medium, it seems that this organization has by now also ceased to exist. Virtually all businesses and most government organizations have made the move by now from microfilm to digital storage, mainly because of the greater versatility of the latter medium for B2B.

20. For the business-to-consumer (B2C)[22] type of e-commerce, however, EDI was not a huge success. The reasons are not hard to find. Instead of the long-term relationship with a few well-trusted business partners, which is typical of B2B, B2C requires one to 'strut one's wares' on the Internet before the eyes of unknown potential buyers. Obviously, the risk factor is much higher and, therefore, greater security precautions also need to be taken.

21. A number of business models exist for B2C e-commerce.[23] These are:

- products sales models, where the electronic retailer directly charges visitors who purchase products or services from the e-commerce website;
- subscription models, where a fixed monthly or annual subscription is charged for the service delivered via the Internet;
- transaction fee models, where a fee is determined on the basis of the volume and value of the transactions;
- advertising-supported models, where revenue is obtained from advertisers and not directly from visitors to the website; and
- sponsorship models, where businesses may sponsor a 'glossy' website for non-financial[24] reasons, because of its advertising value. The site at <www. bmw-.co.za> is a good example.

§3. Development of e-Commerce Through Mobile Devices

22. The biggest provider of published business directories, Braby's, has shifted its focus from mere paper-based information and has thrown its full weight behind a digital venture. For further detail on this pioneering development, *see* www.brabys.com. It seems that a separate venture called www.iFind.co.za no longer exists. *See also* my comments above on the increased penetration of cell phones among South African Blacks and the effect that this is likely to have on the general population.[25]

---

22. Also known as 'e-tailing', *see supra.*
23. *See* Managing E-Commerce at 213–214.
24. At least not directly.
25. *See supra* at para. 18. For the local situation, *see* DP van der Merwe 'Enkele gedagtes oor mobiele handeldryf or m-handel ('m-commerce')' THRHR (2006): 318ff. (Although this note is in Afrikaans it should be readily accessible to Dutch or Flemish-speaking readers).

§4. Internet Banking

23. All the major South African banks have excellent Internet websites, by means of which a variety of virtual banking transactions may be carried out. The fact that a greater proportion of money is being exchanged in 'virtual' format also reduces the chance of violent crime, a phenomenon all too common in this crime-ridden country. Unfortunately, it has also opened the door to a new breed of criminal, namely the 'hacker', who gets access to supposedly 'secure' sites and transfers money electronically to his or her bank account. Related to this is the crime of 'phishing' in which a fraudster pretends to be the organizer of a major lottery, a beneficiary of a fortune in Nigeria, or something similar, in order to obtain vital personal detail from the user. It is, therefore, almost 'theft of information', if such a crime were possible.[26] At worst, the 'phisher' may even persuade an unwitting victim to transfer funds to the phisher's bank account, on the strength of some vaporous promises. This is, of course, fraud, in terms of the common law or as a contravention of section 86 of the South African Electronic Communications and Transactions Act (ECT Act).[27]

24. Electronic funds transfers (EFTs) and (online) credit card payments have significantly increased in South Africa to such an extent that traditional paper cheque payments have now become a thing of the past. That said, most payments on the Internet are still credit card transactions with the attendant risk that this brings because of bogus websites or even because of actions by dishonest employees of generally trusted websites.[28] Hopefully this is but a temporary problem as payment systems become more attuned to the sophisticated possibilities of e- and m-commerce in ensuring sophisticated methods of authentication.

26. In Nigeria this is known as a 'section 419-scan' following the article number in their criminal code.
27. Act 25 of 2002.
28. Van der Merwe et al., *ICT Law* (2022): 229-230.

Chapter 5. e-Government Initiatives

25. Mention has already been made of the ECT Act.[29] This act contains, in one of its first chapters, some major initiatives, with time frames, for e-government to get going in South Africa. Unfortunately, most of these ambitious plans have come to naught, probably because of a change of personnel in the government departments concerned.

26. According to the national e-strategy,[30] the Minister of Communications was required to develop a 'three-year national e-strategy' for South Africa within twenty-four months after the promulgation of the act. Relevant factors in the strategy were supposed to be:

(a) the electronic transactions strategy of the Republic;
(b) programmes and means to achieve universal access, human resource development, and development of SMEs;
(c) programmes and means to promote the overall readiness of the Republic in respect of electronic transactions;
(d) ways to promote the Republic as a preferred provider and user of electronic transactions in the international market;
(e) existing government initiatives directly or indirectly relevant to or impacting on the national e-strategy and, if applicable, how such initiatives are to be utilized in attaining the objectives of the national e-strategy;
(f) the role expected to be performed by the private sector in the implementation of the national e-strategy;
(g) the role expected to be performed by the private sector in the implementation of the national e-strategy and how government can solicit the participation of the private sector to perform such role;
(h) the defined objectives, including time frames within which the objectives are to be achieved;
(i) the resources required to achieve the objectives provided for in the national e-strategy.

27. Upon approval by the Cabinet, the Minister of Communications must publish the national e-strategy in the Gazette.[31] In the fourteen years following the promulgation of the ECT Act, the government has not published a corresponding strategy that the author has been able to trace, and it seems less and less likely that it will ever take place.

28. This is not to say that there have not been some promising e-government initiatives since, particularly towards assisting the overburdened courts. According to a previous Minister of Justice, Ms Brigitte Mabandla, an increased use of ICT technology is a priority for both her department and the 'Justice, Crime Prevention and

29. *Ibid.*
30. Set out in Ch. 2, Part I, s. 5 of the Act.
31. At the time of writing, this has not yet happened.

Security Cluster' (JCPS).[32] Items being implemented soon are: an 'e-Scheduler' case-management system; a digital court-recording system; an audio-visual case postponement closed-circuit television (CCTV) system; a workflow system for the Legal Aid Board; a system connecting the databases of the Department of Justice with the system of the Department of Home Affairs, including the latter department's electronic fingerprinting, as well as an integrated justice system (IJS) data warehouse; and automation of the police-docket system with electronic capturing of the data.[33]

32. Court finally get wired at <www.itweb.co.za/section> (August 2007).
33. Van der Merwe et al., *ICT Law* (2022), 5-6.

Part I. Digital Market Regulation

Chapter 1. Legal Status of Standards and Technical Specifications

§1. Non-binding Self-Regulation

29. Self-regulation is probably the best solution for any industry where standards are of a technical nature and liable to misinterpretation by another field of knowledge as constituted by the law. To some degree, this has been built into the licensing structure for the protection of personal information (for instance, the POPI-Act).[34]

30. Standards are also of great importance for legal certainty, particularly in the field of evidence. Examples of these are data standards such as eXtensible Markup Language (XML) and eXtensible Business Reporting Language (XBRL). The latter standard has brought both flexibility and certainty to the world of electronic commerce, for instance, statutory reports by companies.[35]

34. See Part VIII below.
35. See Van der Merwe et al., *ICT Law* (2022) 146–149.

Chapter 2. Legal Status of Standard Terms and Conditions

§1. The Standard Terms and Conditions of a Contract

31. A 'terms and conditions agreement' is the founding agreement that determines the terms, the rules and other guidelines of behaviour that would be acceptable to all the contracting parties. In case of the Internet and with e-commerce as well as m-commerce, users have to agree to be bound by these conditions in order to gain access to and participate in the activities (usually commercial) set out by the online merchant.

32. Rather than contract with possibly millions of users, an online merchant simply publishes his terms of use on one of the initial electronic pages and gives the potential client the choice to either simply agree to everything or to withdraw from the potential agreement. This does not leave any room for bargaining, 'horse-trading' or anything of this nature.

33. In the work *Information and Communications Technology Law*[36] the different techniques used to incorporate the normal standard terms are differentiated. These terms might form part and parcel of the contract filled in and signed by the parties (for instance, suretyship contracts used by a bank). However, the signed face of a contract might refer to and incorporate the standard terms printed on the reverse side of the document (although this is not really applicable in the electronic environment). More often in the digital world, one might find a reference to standard terms available elsewhere – usually on the company website. Back to the real world, a generally visible sign at the place of contracting would contain the terms of further use – for instance, at parking garages and amusement parks. Finally, a so-called click-wrap-contract is entered upon by merely clicking on a mouse button or even on a keyboard or on the screen itself.

34. *See* also Part VII Chapter 1 below for a more expansive treatment of electronic contracts.

36. See *supra* 198ff.

Chapter 3. International Private Law Applied to the Online Environment

§1. WHAT IS INTERNATIONAL PRIVATE LAW?

35. Also known as 'Conflict of Laws', International Private Law may be described as 'the law governing disputes between citizens (human or corporate) against a foreign country. Disputes in (international) private law are often solved via negotiation, arbitration, litigation or a combination of these'.[37]

36. Perhaps the best (and most easily grasped) exposition of International Private Law that the present author has come across may be found in a work entitled *Legal Aspects of Doing Business in Singapore.*[38] Chapter 10 on 'Venturing Overseas: Legal Aspects'[39] contains section 10.3 entitled 'Private International Law and How it Affects Business'.[40]

37. The author first distinguishes between *private international law* and *public international law* as follows:

> Public international law governs the rights and relationships between nations and among international organisations, such as the United Nations.

38. Later on, he adds an important definition for our present purposes:

> Private international law deals instead with the rights and liabilities as between *private individuals* (whether persons, companies or other entities).

39. He then emphasizes four notable 'key issues' which affect business, namely:

(1) Jurisdiction
(2) Applicable law
(3) The enforcement of foreign judgments
(4) Sovereign immunity.

1 Jurisdiction

40. The fact that parties from different countries might start litigating against each other (an eventuality made much more likely since the arrival of the Internet) has led to the possibility of two legal systems competing for jurisdiction. Certain rules have been framed in this regard (under Latin headings) such as forum non conveniens – which court would be the most convenient to hear the matter, *Lis alibi*

37. See https://guides.law.ufl.edu/website/home (accessed 11th November 2021).
38. Edited by George Shenoy and Toh See Kiat (Addison Wesley) 1996.
39. By Low Kee Yang.
40. From pp. 332–340.

pendens – where has a case progressed the furthest, or finally, a specific foreign jurisdiction clause in a contract might settle the matter.

2 Applicable Law

41. If the parties have made a particular choice in this regard, no further problems should arise. Where no express choice has been exercised, the court will first try to find an implied choice in this regard, such as the language used. Failing this, courts will have to impute a choice to the parties. A problem that might arise in this regard is that something that is legal in one country might not also be legal in another.

3 Enforcement of Foreign Judgments

42. The main problem with this type of litigation only starts after the court has delivered judgment. How can practical effect be given to this judgment? The simplest solution would be if prior reciprocal agreements have been put in place for the signatory countries to enforce each other's judgments. A second solution might be for the judgment enforcing court to recognize a foreign judgment as a debt and to allow the judgment creditor to sue thereon. The author suggests that arbitration might provide another way out of this dilemma.

4 Sovereign immunity

43. Simply put, the problem may arise whether the citizen of one country may successfully sue and recover from a government or governmental agency in another. This problem has been alleviated by changing a position of *absolute* state immunity in this type of case to one of *relative* immunity.

§2. How Does International Private Law Relate to South Africa?

44. In this regard a very useful work is *Private International Law in South Africa,*[41] where the problems elucidated under the previous heading are brought home to a local context. This work makes use, *inter alia,* of another excellent South African source, namely Forsyth's *Private International Law.*[42]

45. The first-mentioned work points out that the common law with regard to Private International Law (PIL) derives from writers on Roman-Dutch law such as Rodenburg, P Voet, J Voet, Huber and Van der Keessel. A large number of South African statutes also relate to PIL.[43] The authors then analyse the 'Rules of Choice of Law' as it relates to Persons (Chapter 1), Obligations (Chapter 2) which may arise

41. By E Schoeman, C Roodt and M Wethmar-Lemmer (Wolters Kluwer) 2014.
42. By C Forsyth (Juta) 4th ed. 2003.
43. *Supra* 17.

from contract or as a result of delict, Law of Property (Chapter 3), Intangible Property Rights (Chapter 4) which might involve Patent Law or Copyright, Family Law (Chapter 6) and Law of Succession (Chapter 7).

46. The work also contains a 'Part III. Annex: International Civil Procedure (ICP)'. It is interesting to note how these procedural issues correspond with the Singaporean 'key issues' discussed above under paragraph 36. For instance, Chapters 3 and 4 of the Annex deal with issues of national and international jurisdiction, respectively. Chapter 5 deals with the more substantive issue of the acceptability (or recognition) and enforcement of foreign judgments. The entire Part II (dealt with in the previous paragraph) deals with the rules of choice of law (or 'applicable law') with regard to the topics mentioned above. However, at first glance, I was unable to find where these authors dealt with the topic of sovereign immunity.

47. As mentioned above, the authors just cited made use of the work Forsyth's *Private International Law*.[44] In the latter work, this author sets out a useful distinction between public international law and private international law:[45]

> Whereas public international law is essentially a supra-national legal order regulating the legal relation between states, each national legal system has its own system of private international law.

48. The author also explains why he prefers calling this subject 'private international law' rather than 'Conflict of Laws', because the latter seems to imply some 'trial of strength' between two legal systems, where the winner will be rewarded by having its legal system applied in a specific case. He does then make copious use of the phrase 'Choice of Law' in the rest of the book. Later on, the author distinguishes between various fields of law where a court may have to determine exactly which legal system should be applicable. Chapter 7[46] concentrates on 'The Family and Choice of Law: and distinguishes between Part One which deals with 'Husband and Wife' and Part Two dealing with 'Children.'

49. Chapter 8[47] deals with 'Choice of Law in Cases involving Legal Obligations' and then distinguishes between Contractual obligations in Part One and Delictual Obligations in Part Two. Part Three covers Choice of Law and Unjust Enrichment.

50. Chapter 10 covers 'The Recognition and Enforcement of Foreign Judgments'. The reader should recognize this topic immediately since both sources mentioned in the first part of this chapter have also devoted considerable attention to this

---

44. By C Forsyth (Juta) 4th ed. 2003.
45. *Supra* 4.
46. *Supra* 260ff.
47. *Supra* 293ff.

topic. Under this heading Forsyth deals with 'international competence' for claims sounding in money, international competence in matrimonial actions and the same in judgments relating to property.

51. To summarize, even though the principles of International Private Law have become reasonably clear-cut, their application to an ever-increasing digital world is not yet that clear. The 'World Wide Web' means exactly that, and lawyers worldwide now have to try and marry disparate legal systems to each other. Again a bilateral or multi-lateral treaty between related governments would seem to be the best solution.

Chapter 4. Competition Law Applied to the Digital Market

52. In this relatively recent field of law, one of the best analyses of the South African position has been carried out by B. Strunz in his work *The Interface of Competition Law, Industrial Policy and Development: The Case of South Africa.*[48] Unfortunately, for purposes of the present work, he does not devote a separate section to the influence of and the effect on information technology, and one has to carefully sift through the above-mentioned (and rather lengthy) work to find these. The present author will endeavour to introduce such references below.

53. In Part I, Strunz deals with 'The Foundations of Industrial Policy and Competition Law'. The author contrasts a government's development policy with the relevant principles of competition law and indicates that a conflict might arise between these two goals.[49] He also draws an interesting comparison between the varied approaches taken between different groupings of countries to competition law.[50] In the United States, for instance, their principles of competition are efficiency based. By contrast, most countries in Europe take a more structuralist approach. Many Third World countries, however, suffer from efficiency concerns due to factors such as corruption and other problems pertaining to distribution. He classifies South Africa into this third group: despite its membership in intra-national groupings such as Brazil, Russia, India, China and South Africa (BRICS), South Africa cannot yet (or no longer[51]) be seen as a 'major emerging economy'.

54. One of the sure signs of a country falling within this third group would be the over-important role assigned to state-owned enterprises (SOEs). Strunz describes the latter in less than flattering terms: 'SOEs are large behemoths rather than mid-sized businesses.'[52] These organizations enjoy protection from competition, receive financial support from the state irrespective of their economic performance and are even exempt from bankruptcy. They are not accountable to taxpayers who are really the 'effective shareholders'! All of these factors constitute a 'distortion of competition in particular'. This would not simply be a negative development provided that it served developmental goals, almost always important in a Third World country. 'Whilst for many protecting competition may be worthwhile per se, in developing countries this may be seen as an intermediate goal that helps the ultimate goal of development.'[53]

55. In Part II, Strunz deals with 'Competition Law, Industrial Policy and South Africa'. The author distinguishes a certain group of countries where technology and innovation play a major role with regard to their markets. In this group (which unfortunately does not include South Africa), 'competition should be analysed with

48. Munich Studies on Innovation and Competition (2018).
49. *Supra* 5.
50. *Supra* 12.
51. Slightly cynical remark by the present commentator.
52. *Supra* 44ff.
53. *Supra* 51.

regard to its dynamic aspects'.[54] He indicates how locally the mix of government interference in businesses and its racial policies during the reign of the National Party have resulted in laws inimical to free competition. In State-owned organizations, such as the electricity supplier Escom and Sasol (the fuel extractor from coal), the idea was to increase South Africa's independence from overseas imports. Nonetheless, practices such as the 'dominance of foreign capital' and the 'use of black labour' persisted and continued to grow.[55] In this type of organization (which is reliant on State support) 'protectionist tariff policy could not be rescinded once it had become part of the industrial policy landscape'.[56]

56. In the post-Apartheid era (starting from May 1994), the now governing African National Congress (ANC) hoped some of the successful policies adopted by many of the recently independent East Asian countries. This was limited by the new government's 'Growth, Employment and Redistribution' (GEAR) strategy to aid previously disenfranchised non-white South African citizens.[57] After 2004 efforts at privatization have mostly stalled and state intervention had once again become more prominent. In a development unique to South Africa, the sole focus was no longer on economic growth. On the production side, a new focus arose on services and human capabilities approach – the latter concentrating not only on growth but also on 'social transformation'.[58] This meant that Rivest-Shamir-Adleman (RSA) has turned into a 'classic welfare state' with a lack of focus on growth, no suppression of labour in the interests of such growth, too high wages, a non-efficient bureaucracy and a non-submissive civil society.[59] Fortunately, an enforcement priority was seen to be the need to develop an adequate IT network with the necessary infrastructure.[60]

57. The area of competition law in South Africa is governed by the Competition Act[61] which came into effect on 1 September 1999. It forbids certain restrictive practices and relationships in both a horizontal and a vertical sense. The former would include illegal cartels, market allocations and also bid rigging. Nonetheless, the act also makes provision for an 'Efficiency' defence. The latter would include a practice within the different levels of the distribution chain (for instance, between supplier, company and customer) as such practice 'substantially lessens competition'.[62] A company would be penalized not simply for being large but for being large and then abusing its size to increase its market power. According to Strunz, the act's 'procedural rights paired with a thoughtful consideration of opposing interests have

54. *Supra* 105.
55. *Supra* 118.
56. *Supra* 122.
57. *Supra* 125.
58. *Supra* 137ff.
59. *Supra* 140.
60. *Supra* 133.
61. Act 89 of 1998.
62. *Supra* 155.

made interpreting the law a laborious and lengthy task'.[63] He then examines a number of South African organizations that have brought litigation before the court. These cases include *Telkom, Arcelor, Sasol, Foskor, South African Airways, Senwes, Patensie Co-operative* and *South African Breweries*. From an IT-perspective, the *South African Airways* (SAA) case was interesting because of its use of 'extensive economic data'. In the end, both the Competition Tribunal and Appeal Court held that the SAA was an example of anti-competitive behaviour by the government. It was a company in state hands which the government simply refused to give up for political reasons 'although it is inefficient, running losses and in need of billions each year'.[64]

58. In the opinion of Strunz, more than sixteen years of case law following upon the inception of the Competition Act has created a solid body of case law with the factor of public interest playing an important role in most cases.[65] He finishes his examination of the legal position in South Africa with the following conclusion: 'The above results display the complexity of the interface between competition law, industrial policy and developmental concerns.'[66]

59. He ends his work with a useful listing of mergers where the principles of competition law were considered. As may be gleaned from some of the parties involved, many of them were engaged in the practice of cyberlaw in the wider sense. Companies such as Dimension Data, MWeb, Bytes Technology, Telkom SA, Cell C and Altech Autopage all form part of this panoply.

60. In one of the latest South African works on this topic that the present author was able to find,[67] Dr Precious Ndlovu reaffirms many of the aspects dealt with above. It does still remain a detailed search, however, to find any aspects of her work on Competition Law overlapping with the title of the present work, namely *Cyberlaw*.

61. One aspect which does show promise is the factor of 'technological gains' mentioned in section 5(2) of the Competition Act. Even upon analysing the numerous decided cases mentioned by Ndlovu, the specific content of this wide term remains nebulous.

62. An important legal concept which does emerge from an overview of South African case law is that of 'characterization', a concept judicially deduced from the provisions of section 4(1)(b) of the Competition Act. The first such case was *American National Soda Ash Corporation v. Competition Commission and Others*.[68] Here the court laid down the test for characterization as follows:

---

63. *Supra* 180.
64. *Supra* 266.
65. *Supra* 333.
66. *Supra* 444.
67. *Competition Law in South Africa* by PN Ndlovu (Wolters Kluwer 2018).
68. 2005 (3) [All SA] 1 (SCA).

> It is to establish whether the character of the conduct complained of coincides with the character of the prohibited conduct: and this process necessarily embodies two elements. One is the scope of the prohibition: a matter of statutory construction. The is the nature of the conduct complained of: this is a factual enquiry. In ordinary language this can be termed 'characterizing' the conduct – the term used in the United States, which ANSAC[69] has adopted.

63. Applying this characterization test to the facts of the case, the Appellate Division referred the case back to the tribunal to first determine the scope of the prohibition contained in subsection 4(1)(b) and second to decide on the admissibility of evidence led by American Natural Soda Ash Corporation (ANSAC) and whether this would help this party to prove its case. In other words, whether ANSAC had succeeded in 'characterizing' its defence both as far as determining the scope of the prohibition and proving whether the specific conduct of one of the parties would fall within such prohibition.

64. The ANSAC case was followed by a number of other South African cases dealing with this new characterization test in South African Competition Law. An excellent discussion of these (as well as with the ANSAC case) may be found in an article entitled 'The Development of Characterization in South African Competition Law'.[70] The author analyses a number of cases in this regard as will be set out below.

65. The first of these was *Competition Commission v. South African Breweries*[71] decided by the Competition Appeal Court (CAC). The Commission alleged that South African Breweries (SAB) had committed 'market allocation' by appointing distributors with 'exclusive territory agreements'. This would contravene section 4(1)(b)(ii) of the Competition Act. The CAC held that the main test was whether the relationship between SAB and its distributors was of a horizontal nature (which might easily lead to a suspicion of direct or indirect fixing of purchase and/or selling prices) or of a vertical nature, which meant that competition was not excluded upfront. The CAC found the latter possibility. Even though the SAB had its own distribution network, this did not preclude other distribution networks from also distributing SAB goods.

66. A subsequent decision on the issue of characterization was *Dawn Consolidated Holdings and Others v. the Competition Commission.*[72] The matter turned on a shareholding agreement between Dawn (Dawn) and Warplas Share Trust (WST) in respect of High Density Polyethelene Pipes (HDPE) manufactured by Sangio Pipes. One clause of the agreement restrained Dawn from manufacturing HDPE

69. American Natural Soda Ash Corporation (present author's note).
70. Authored by S Strachan and published in *Pricing and Distribution* on 4/10/2019.
71. 129/CAC/Apr2014.
72. 155/CAC/Oct2017.

piping in South Africa for as long as Dawn had a shareholding in Sangio. The CAC used a threefold test in order to decide whether characterization was applicable in the present instance:

1. Is the main agreement, minus the impugned restraint unobjectionable from a competition law perspective?
2. If so, is the restraint reasonably required for the conclusion and implementation of the main agreement?
3. If so, is the restraint reasonably proportionate to the requirement served.[73]

67. Applying this threefold test, the CAC held first that the main agreement was unobjectionable, second that the restraint was enforceable and reasonably required for the agreement between Dawn and WST and third, as far as proportionality was concerned, that the restraint only existed as long as Dawn was a shareholder of Sangio and therefore fell within reasonable limits.

68. Having applied the above test to the facts of the matter, the CAC found that an initial finding by the Competition Commission that the transaction would amount to market allocation in terms of section 4(1)(b)(ii) was not correct. An appeal by Dawn and WTS was therefore upheld.

69. A final case worth mentioning is that of *A'Africa Pest Prevention CC (A'Africa) v. The Competition Commission.*[74] The matter turned on a suspicion of collusive tendering between A'Africa and Mosebetsi Mmoho Professional Services (Mosebetsi). Seeing that both firms were effectively being run by a Ms Labuschagne and each submitted virtually identical tenders. The Commission and the Tribunal held that this constituted collusive tendering in contravention of section 4(1)(b)(iii) of the Competition Act. However, both A'Africa and Mosebetsi appealed to the CAC, partly on the grounds that the previous forums had not fully taken into account the principle of characterization. The CAC found that because Ms Labuschagne had, in effect, no colluding partner, she could not collude with herself and that the complaint by the Commission could be dismissed.

70. In an interesting overview of the above-mentioned decisions, Strachan finds that in ANSAC and Dawn, the conduct of the firms was characterized by the courts; in SAB the economic relationship between the firms was characterized by the CAC and in A'Africa the management and control of the firms (as well as the conduct) was characterized by the CAC. He finds characterization to be important as it allows conduct to be classified, on the one hand, as 'so egregious that no defence should be entertained'. On the other hand, it 'ensures that competition law does not unnecessarily hamper or obstruct pro-competitive and genuine commercial transactions from occurring, and allows courts to avoid false positives'.

---

73. Wording of test taken from the Strachan article mentioned in a previous footnote.
74. 168/CAC/Oct2018.

Chapter 5. Regulation of the Electronic Communications Market (Telecommunications Law)

§1. Background

71. According to the old South African Telecommunications Act,[75] the term 'telecommunication' means the emission, transmission, or reception of a signal from one point to another by means of electricity, magnetism, radio or other electromagnetic waves, or any agency of a like nature, whether with or without the aid of tangible conductors.

72. Unfortunately, the telecommunications sector in South Africa has been a government-sponsored monopoly for many years, held by a company called Telkom. After the first elections held in terms of universal suffrage in 1994, the African National Congress (ANC) became the governing party. Their policy was to allow Telkom a further monopoly for a limited period in order to roll out services to previously disadvantaged (mainly black, coloured, and Indian) communities. The monopoly has since come to an end, and Neotel,[76] the SNO, was in operation for about twelve years. In this regard, *see* Chapter 2 paragraph 10 above.

73. For many years, the above-mentioned Telecommunications Act and its forerunners were the only directly relevant legislation in this area. The age of this act shows in the fact that the word 'Internet' is not even defined in its definition section. This blind eye towards one of the most important technological innovations of the past few decades has led to much uncertainty in this area and to some litigation against the monopolistic national service provider. In 2002, the South African Department of Communications (DOC), then headed by a dynamic Director General,[77] sponsored an ECT Act,[78] which finally brought South Africa (and even the continent of Africa) into the age of electronic commerce. This was followed by legislation[79] that concentrated more specifically on the provision of electronic communication services and their convergence and which will be discussed in greater detail below. All these acts form but part of a panoply of telecommunications-related legislation, which will be described under the following heading.

§2. Legal Framework

74. Mention has already been made in the previous paragraph of the (old) South African Telecommunications Act, the (then new) Electronic Communications Act,

75. Act 103 of 1996.
76. <www.neotel.co.za>.
77. Andile Ngcaba, who has since unfortunately been snatched up by the private sector.
78. Act 25 of 2002. Most of its criminal provisions have now been subsumed and rewritten by Act 19 of 2020 (see Part VI below).
79. The Electronic Communications Act 36 of 2005.

and the ECT Act. In addition, South Africa passed a Promotion of Access to Information Act (PROATIA).[80] The purpose of the latter act is to give effect to a provision in the South African Constitution[81] that guarantees its citizens the right of access to information which they might need to exercise or protect their rights. This right extends both to any information held by the state and to information held by another person. A counterpart to this may be found in section 14 of the Constitution, which guarantees a right of privacy to everyone, including 'the right not to have the privacy of their communications infringed'. This right to privacy will be discussed below under Part VIII, Chapter 1, paragraphs 538 ff..

75. In order to provide for an honest brokerage between the government and its citizens as far as electronic communications are concerned, the Independent Communications Authority of South Africa (ICASA) Act[82] has just created such an authority. This body has had to struggle to solve problems between Telkom and telecommunications users, probably caused by inadequacies in the Telecommunications and the PROATIA Acts but also by the fact that the two previous problem-solving bodies were too tightly bound up with their historical and technological past. They were governed by the South African Telecommunications Regulatory Authority (SATRA) and the Independent Broadcasting Authority (IBA), respectively. Both of these have now been totally absorbed into ICASA.[83] This indicates the convergence between the former telecommunications and broadcasting control bodies, respectively. Legislation has also been passed to deal with the interception of communications. This is the 'Regulation of Interception of Communications and Provision of Communication-Related Information Act'[84] (ROICAPOCRIA or simply, the RIC Act). These and other laws, as well as the South African common law, will be discussed in greater detail below under their appropriate headings.

76. As has already been mentioned, the old Telecommunications Act[85] has now (almost) completely been replaced in function by the later Electronic Communications Act.[86] The only parts that remain in force are certain regulations in terms of the older act and some licences that have not yet been superseded by licensing in terms of the later act. The Electronic Communications (EC) Act concentrates on putting in place a new licensing regime, which will be further expounded upon under the next heading.

77. The latter act has been described as 'perhaps the most dramatic "event" for telecommunications in South Africa during the last decade'.[87] This piece of legislation has brought about much wider definitions of concepts such as 'electronic communications service', namely:

---

80. The Promotion of Access to information (PROATIA) Act 2 of 2000.
81. Act 108 of 1996.
82. Act 13 of 2000.
83. *See* Van der Merwe et al., *ICT Law* (2022), 18–19.
84. The RIC Act 70 of 2002.
85. Act 103 of 1996.
86. The EC Act 36 of 2005.
87. Van der Merwe et al., *ICT Law* (2022), 34.

> any service provided to the public, sections of the public, the state, or subscribers to such service, which consists wholly or mainly of the convergence of electronic communications over an electronic communications network, but excludes broadcasting services.[88]

78. Equally important, the key concept of 'electronic communications' is defined as follows:

> the emission, transmission or reception of information, including without limitation, voice, sound, data, text, video, animation, visual images, moving images and pictures, signals or a combination thereof, by means of magnetism, radio or other electromagnetic waves, optical electromagnetic systems or any agency of a like nature, whether with or without the aid of tangible conduct, but does not include content service.[89]

79. It is interesting to note that the definitions of 'electronic communications' and 'information system' partially overlap when one compares the definitions between the EC Act[90] and the ECT Act.[91] Perhaps confusion might be avoided if one reads each act within its own context and field of application, namely electronic commerce and electronic communications, respectively, but the names of the two acts remain open to confusion.[92]

80. In her national contribution to *The International Comparative Legal Guide to Telecommunications Laws and Regulations* (*South Africa*),[93] Lisa Thornton welcomed the moving together of the legal regimes for telecommunications and broadcasting brought about by the EC Act. She did sound one cautionary note about bureaucratic delays, however:

> Movements in this direction, however, will continue to be slowed due to the conflicting roles played by the South African government as policy maker, regulator and competitive service provider.[94]

81. The South African legislature has also passed two important acts to protect the consumer against over-borrowing and also against being tricked into buying inferior products in the marketplace. These acts are the National Credit Act[95] and the Consumer Protection Act.[96] Together these two acts form a valuable shield against the many temptations offered by unscrupulous vendors by means of the Internet.

---

88. Section 1 of Act 36 of 2005.
89. *Ibid.*
90. Act 36 of 2005.
91. Act 25 of 2002.
92. *See also* Van der Merwe et al., *ICT Law* (2022), 36.
93. Global Legal Group (2009).
94. Lisa Thornton, *The International Comparative Legal Guide to Telecommunications Laws and Regulations (South Africa)* (Global Press, 2009), 251 at 256.
95. Act 34 of 2005. *See* Van der Merwe et al., *ICT Law* (2022) 473ff.
96. Act 68 of 2008. *See* Van der Merwe et al., *ICT Law* (2022) 214ff. and 475ff.

82. In addition, the long-awaited statutory protection of privacy has now come about in the shape of Protection of Personal Information Act.[97] This will be further discussed under Part VIII below.

§3. Licensing Regime

83. In terms of the above-mentioned Telecommunications Act,[98] no person could provide a telecommunications service except under and in accordance with a telecommunication service licence issued to that person in terms of that act. It was envisaged that Telkom and Neotel would initially be the only holders of public switched telecommunication service licences although the length of Telkom's monopoly actually exceeded expectations by a fair amount. The Minister of Telecommunications may now grant additional public switched telecommunication service licences and at least one of the additional operator has been licensed to provide service-based competition. It is also interesting that all new licences will have to be granted in terms of, and according to, the conditions set by the EC Act.

84. On 7 May 2002, a South African firm called Sentech Limited was granted a licence to provide 'an international telecommunication gateway service enabling it to operate as a carrier of carriers' as well as 'multimedia services to any person who requests such service'. Sentech is supposed to provide the latter service to any person who requests such service 'as a common carrier on a reasonable, equitable and non-discriminatory basis'.[99]

85. One might say that the key provisions of the EC Act are those dealing with the later licensing framework.[100] These provisions are all contained in Chapter 3 of the act in which a number of sections will be emphasized. Section 7, for instance, provides that no communications services may be rendered, unless in terms of a valid licence issued in terms of the Act. Section 6 provides for certain exemptions in terms of the same act. These are for electronic communications services provided on a not-for-profit basis, by resellers, on private networks or on local area networks. Section 5 forms the 'meat' of this part of the act and describes the new licensing process in detail.

86. Certain of the concepts relevant to section 5 have already been defined above.

---

97. Act 4 of 2014, also known as the POPI Act. *See* Van der Merwe et al., *ICT Law* (2022) 476ff.
98. Act 103 of 1996 ss 32 and 32A.
99. Section 32C
100. Van der Merwe et al., *ICT Law* (2022), 32.

§4. LIBERALIZATION OF THE TELECOMMUNICATIONS SECTOR

87. As may be gathered from the foregoing sections, Telkom enjoyed an uninterrupted monopoly for many years. It was hoped that a second regime or SNO and other role players would help to liberalize this sector. The SNO was licensed on 9 December 2005 and was made up of a number of constituent companies such as Nexus Connections, Tata (Africa), Eskom, and Transnet and started trading as Neotel.[101] In May 2014, a buyout offer from the cellular operator Vodacom was accepted, but it has since been incorporated into Liquid Intelligent Technologies as of October 2016.

88. A number of mobile cellular telecommunication operators have been licensed, and the role players in other categories in the world of telecommunications are also starting to increase. The issue of 4G and Long Term Evolution (LTE) licences have become common and even the Fifth Generation (of cellular technology) (5G) standard has now really arrived in South Africa (although some fears exist that the latter might interfere with certain types of communication and might even present a health risk).

101. *See* <www.neotel.co.za>.

Chapter 6. Regulation of Broadcasting Activities (Audio-Visual Services)

89. Traditionally broadcasting has been dealt with in a different fashion from mail and telecommunication services.[102] Nowadays, information technology should probably be added to the 'convergence' spectrum of communication services.

90. In South Africa, these matters were formerly dealt with by means of a (now repealed) Broadcasting Act.[103] Because of the convergence of technologies, even broadcasting is now dealt with by means of the EC Act.[104]

91. Quite important is the definition of 'broadcasting' in the EC Act, which is defined as:

> any form of unidirectional electronic communication intended for reception by:
>
> a) the public;
> b) sections of the public;
> c) subscribers to any broadcasting service,
>
> whether conveyed by means of radio frequency spectrum or any electronic communications network or any combination thereof and 'broadcast' is constructed accordingly.[105]

92. The act also proceeds to distinguish between individual and class licences, and these names, as well as some other concepts dealt with, are fairly self-explanatory.[106]

---

102. *See* Van der Merwe et al., *ICT Law* (2022) 15ff.
103. Act 4 of 1999.
104. Act 36 of 2005 (henceforth referred to as the EC Act)..
105. Section 1 of Act 36 of 2005.
106. *See* s. 5(3) and 5(5) (of the same Act) respectively.

Chapter 7. Regulation of Online Interactive Services (e-Commerce)

§1. General Background

93. This chapter covers the mere legislative aspects of the important growth area of electronic commerce (EC). For facts and figures, the reader should *see* Chapter 4 under General Introduction *supra*. For a substantive discussion of the specific advantages (and dangers) of contracting online, the reader is directed to Part III, Chapter 1 below: 'Online Contracting'.

§2. Regulation of Online Interactive Services

94. Electronic commerce has been a worldwide phenomenon requiring universal solutions. Therefore the United Nations Commission on International Trade Law (UNCITRAL) enacted a Model Law in this regard in 1996. South Africa has adopted most of these provisions in its own ECT Act.[107] Subsection 11(1) determines that such contracting may take place by means of data messages. Section 22 enhances this provision by determining that no agreement shall be considered invalid merely because it was formed wholly, or in part by means of data messages.

107. Act 25 of 2002.

Chapter 8. Regulation of Cryptography in South Africa

§1. General Background

95. From the Greek language, we have inherited the words *kryptos* (meaning hidden) and *logos* (meaning word). The process of cryptography, therefore, means (literally) 'to write word(s) that are hidden from. As in most other countries that have embarked upon the e-commerce and m-commerce route, adequate security is of the utmost importance. This type of security is needed in order to win over reluctant new participants in these processes. The most widely used method to achieve the required standard of security is to make use of cryptography in order to encrypt the messages that form the backbone of any electronic commercial process. Two bills following the pattern of the ECT Act (discussed above) have placed considerable emphasis on security. The first originated from the Department of Communications in 2012, but there is no indication when (if ever) it would come into operation.[108] The same applies to a 2015 Bill from the Department of Justice.[109] Whereas the first tries to follow the pattern set by the ECT Act, the latter bill concentrates on criminal law and procedure, but especially on cybersecurity. In the latter regard, an entire bureaucracy is envisaged comprising a 'Cyber Security Centre' and a 'Cyber Response Committee' forming part of a 'Cyber Security Hub'. A much-needed improvement would be the 24/7 contact centre required by the 2001 Budapest Convention.[110]

§2. Regulation of Cryptography in South Africa

96. Perhaps because of its apartheid background, South Africa has not been party to any of the international instruments governing the use of cryptography.[111] Instead, South Africa has made extensive military use of cryptography and has provided for the import and export of this technology by means of the Defence Armament and Protection Act[112] and the General Armaments Control Schedule[113] in terms of that act.

97. It was left to the ECT Act[114] to regulate civil cryptography in South Africa, particularly the ways in which this technology affects private commercial activities. Chapter 5 of this act deals with cryptography and section 1 of the act contains several important definitions in this regard. The Department of Communication has also since published important regulations governing cryptography[115] to govern the procedure for a cryptography provider who wishes to register in terms of the act.

108. GN 888 in Government Gazette 35821 of 16 Oct. 2012.
109. B 2015 from the Minister of Justice and Correctional Services.
110. *See* further in this regard Van der Merwe et al., *ICT Law* (2016), 132–133.
111. *See* further in this regard, Snail, Papadopoulos (eds.), *Cyberlaw@SA* III (2012), 323.
112. Act 57 of 1968.
113. Published in Regulation Gazette R888 on 13 May 1994.
114. Act 25 of 2000.
115. GN R216 in GG 28594 of 10 Mar. 2006.

These govern information to be supplied with each application, for instance, any outsourcing of cryptography services as well as information about any trusted personnel providing supervisory or management services.[116]

98. A 'cryptography product' is defined by the act as:

> any product that:
>
> – makes use of cryptographic techniques
> – is used by a sender or recipient of data messages
>
> for the purposes of ensuring
> that such data can be accessed only by relevant persons;
> the authenticity of the data;
> the integrity of the data;
> that the source of the data can be correctly ascertained.

99. Finally, a 'cryptography service' is defined as:

> any service which is provided to a sender or a recipient of a data message or to anyone storing a data message, and which is designed to facilitate the use of cryptographic techniques for the purpose of ensuring –
>
> that such data or data message can be accessed or can be put into an intelligible form only by certain persons;
> that the authenticity or integrity of such data or data message is capable of being ascertained;
> the integrity of the data or data message;
> that the source of the data or data message can be correctly ascertained.

100. A 'cryptography provider' is defined as 'any person who provides or who proposes to provide cryptography services or products in the Republic'. The Director General of the DOC has to establish and maintain a register of cryptography providers.[117]

101. This last measure has attracted a fair amount of criticism. Keeping the register itself requires that sufficient details concerning the cryptography provider must

116. *See also* Van der Merwe et al., *ICT Law* (2022), 144ff on Cryptography Regulation and New Concept Legislation.
117. Section 29(1) of Act 25 of 2002.

be recorded, in order that such provider (or its products or services) may be identified and located. This requirement has worried the users of 'open-source' software[118] because such software often has no single owner of distributor. Would this mean that open-source cryptography products cannot be registered (and, therefore, not used) in South Africa?

102. According to Wim Mostert,[119] the statutory requirement for registration serves the following purpose. In terms of the RIC Act,[120] certain powers may be exercised by the statutory authorities, and these authorities might need the above-mentioned particulars in order to request a decryption key from the registrant in terms of a 'decryption direction'. This type of direction will only be issued by a judge who is satisfied that a 'decryption key-holder' is really in possession of the encrypted information and the specific decryption key thereto.

103. The situation prescribed for South Africa reminds one of the infamous clipper chip, which former US President Clinton tried to get prescribed by statute in the US. This chip was required to be built with a 'back-door', through which only properly authorized government officials would have been able to gain access to the information 'encrypted' by the clipper chip. Perhaps as an example to South Africa, the draft US provision met with such determined legislative opposition that it had to be withdrawn in the end. The same battle between state security interests and those of citizens in their privacy has recently manifested in the show-down between James Comey, director of the Federal Bureau of Investigation (FBI), and the Apple Computer Company. The latter refused to provide the former with a 'back-door' which the government might use to access Apple cell phones at its own discretion.[121]

104. Section one of the Regulation of interception of Communications (RIC) Act itself defines a 'decryption key holder' as 'any person who is in possession of a decryption key for purposes of subsequent decryption of encrypted information relating to indirect communications'.

105. The term 'decryption key' is in turn defined as:

> any key, mathematical formula, code, password, algorithm or any other data which is used to:
>
> > allow access to encrypted information; or
> > facilitate the putting of encrypted information into an intelligible form.

118. Such as the LINUX operating system, for instance.
119. Chairperson of the drafting committee for the ECT Act.
120. Act 70 of 2002.
121. *See TIME* magazine of 7 Mar. 2016 18–19 for 'The real meaning of Apple's battle with the FBI over encryption.'

106. The effect of the RIC Act on constitutional rights (such as privacy) still has to be tested in terms of the South African Constitution.[122] Doubt has also been expressed as to whether all this legislative activity will serve any useful purpose:

> The dilemma one faces is that although some, and might be added, few cryptography providers possess an overriding key, most known and used providers are abstaining from such practices and are therefore not in possession or control of any keys issued. The fact is that it is the end users who are in possession of these keys. This would therefore mean that, in terms of the Act, the providers cannot be directed to provide assistance, thereby defeating the very purpose of registering cryptography providers in terms of the ECT Act.[123]

107. Of course, cryptography also plays an important role with regard to modern authentication and electronic signatures. This evidential aspect will be explored more fully under Part III below, where Chapters 2 and 3 deals specifically with the law of evidence and proof, under which heading electronic communications and the attendant evidential problems will be dealt with in greater detail.

108. Unfortunately, in the cryptography regulations[124] now applicable in terms of the South African ECT Act,[125] reference has been made only to the X 509 standard as well as to the security standard SABS/ISO 17799. It can only be hoped that a future amendment will also incorporate some of the international standards mentioned above, especially as far as the use being made of the XML standard with regard to electronic signatures is concerned.

109. The very latest standard in this regard is called eXtensible Business Reporting Language (XBRL) which also derives from the same original system of Standard Generalized Markup Language (SGML) as do those mentioned in the previous paragraphs. Because the XBRL system has tremendous commercial potential, many countries have moved to this standard for their banking and other commercial transactions. Further reading on this subject is strongly recommended and a good start might be an article by the present author,[126] as well as a treatment in context with other markup languages in a recently published work by the same author.[127]

110. The latest iteration of the South African Cybercrime Act,[128] the greater part of which has been signed into law as of 1 of December 2021, confers certain powers upon the authorities investigating cybercrime to search, access or seize articles relevant to a successful prosecution. Such articles might often contain encrypted

122. Act 108 of 1996.
123. Buys (ed.), *Cyberlaw@SA* (2004), 119.
124. GN R216 in GG 28594 of 10 Mar. 2006.
125. Act 25 of 2002.
126. *See* 'XBRL and the Law: Implications of Markup Languages' in 2011 *Journal of Contemporary Roman-Dutch Law (JCR-DL)* 418ff for a detailed exposition.
127. Van der Merwe et al., *ICT Law* (2022), 64ff and 146ff.
128. Act 19 of 2020.

data which would require skills and talent in this aspect from the prosecuting authorities. One can only hope that the South African Police Service (SAPS) would have such expertise at its disposal.

111. Of course, cryptography is an excellent example of 'dual-use' goods, that is, products that might find application in both civil and military use. Being able to send messages that are undecipherable by interceptors in an unfriendly country would be a necessity both for espionage during peacetime and for military intelligence during wartime. Other examples would be IT-driven spy planes (or even unmanned bombing drones), expert systems whose 'wisdom' exceeds a whole panel of human experts and similar applications. In desperate military situations a country might decide to invoke emergency measures in terms of martial law, which would suspend normal law, at least temporarily.

Part II. Online Public Services

Chapter 1. e-Government Legal Framework

112. In November 2007, the South African Department of Telecommunications and Postal Services published an interesting 'National e-government Strategy and Roadmap'.[129] It is useful and enlightening to now review that strategy and to try and evaluate to what extent its noble goals have been achieved. Despite the noble goals stated in the above title, e-health online voting and similar services have not yet received much attention from the South African legislature.

113. In the *Introduction,* the main purpose of this framework is admirably defined: 'to guide the digital transformation of the public service in South Africa into an inclusive digital society where all citizens can benefit from applications offered by digital technologies to improve their quality of life'. The State Information Technology Agency (SITA) is to be the vehicle enabling a suitable ICT environment for government departments to provide e-services to its citizens. After explaining some e-government acronyms, the Introduction traces the evolution of e-government in South Africa. It also sets out the international benchmarking of stages in the evolution of such a roll-out. The first stage consists of 'emerging information services' which simply involves static information from government websites. The second stage comprises 'enhanced information services' which would entail government services enhanced by means of either one-way or 'simple' two-way interaction with citizens. Third, would see the emergence of 'transactional services' which would make two-way interaction between government and citizens possible. Finally, 'connected services' should follow with government web pages inviting interaction with citizens, government agencies being 'citizen-centric' and government services being 'customer-centric'.

114. Gauging the success of the South African government according to the above goals, government might argue that it has already achieved the fourth goal as set out above. Unfortunately, the prevalence of crime in South Africa, both online and physically at information kiosks, has complicated matters in this country.

115. In a *Problem Statement* the document does set out the challenges hindering the adoption of e-government in South Africa. These form a list comprising (a) the

129. Notice 886 of 10/11/2017 published in ss 5(5) of the ECT Act 25 of 2002.

lack of synchronization between government departments themselves; (b) large-scale incompatibilities and inefficiencies between departments; (c) the fragmentation of government initiatives; (d) no dedicated budget allocations; (e) diverse applications, platforms, software and databases between different departments; (f) no collaboration between departments, perhaps because no one specific entity has been tasked with leading and managing e-government implementation in this country and (g) the growth and mushrooming of the South African population.

116. The *Vision and Mission* for e-government is stated as: 'to digitise government services while transforming South Africa into an inclusive digital society and economy'.

117. Following on the above, the *Strategic Objectives* are set out as, *inter alia*, 'skills development', as well as a 'one-stop service portal' in order to achieve 'integrated electronic services'. Another (noble) goal should be 'empowering rural and traditionally underserved communities using information and communication technologies'.

118. Also interesting are the *Major Initiatives of an e-Government Service*. The most important are stated to be a 'Batho Pele' ('People First') gateway between government and the public, a central portal in this regard, common cloud ICT architecture, a multi-factor authentication mechanism, a national e-identity structure as well as a reliable 'PKI' (Public Key Infrastructure') to enable reliable e-commerce interaction.

119. The requirements for an *ICT Infrastructure for e-Government Services* are stated to be that it should be robust, easier and cheaper to use than previous alternatives and that security and privacy should be made a priority.

120. A concept *High-Level Implementation Plan* is also mooted. In order to implement this, several key amendments to the South African ECT Act (25 of 2002) as well as to the Public Service Act (103 of 1994) need to be carried out.

121. This instructive report is capped with a very useful *Risk Analysis and Mitigations* concerning the possible problems attendant upon an extensive roll-out of e-government in South Africa.

Part III. Online Transactions

Chapter 1. Online Contracting (Including Smart Contracts and Blockchain)

122. Contracting (buying and selling) has been with us for a very long time. However, it is only in comparatively recent times that it has been possible to carry out such transactions online.

123. All South African banks (as well as other businesses) now have websites whereas the former also operate from standalone kiosks[130] and even from cellular telephones. Cheques and negotiable instruments have been phased out in favour of online business (and perhaps also because the South African Post Office's surface mail system has by now virtually ceased to function). Unfortunately, criminals have now gained IT-skills and are using these as the mechanism to defraud online customers, both locally and overseas.

124. Roman-Dutch law still constitutes the common law for South Africa's law of contract, and these principles of substantive law would still prevail notwithstanding the fact that computer-specific legislation (such as the ECT Act) might determine questions of adjective law.

125. The entire Chapter 6 of *ICT Law*[131] discusses the development of e-commerce, how Electronic Document Interchange (EDI) has come to the fore but has now fallen out of fashion[132] and the elements of contracting safely online, including automated contracts. The result has given rise to the name of 'smart contracts'. Care should, however, also be given by contractants to the international standards as set out by the UNCITRAL Law on Electronic Signatures in this regard.[133]

130. Although nowadays the more reliable 'hole in the wall' installations are preferred since they are less vulnerable to 'bank' robbers.
131. *See* Van der Merwe et al., *ICT Law* (2022) Chapter 6 161ff
132. Except in the case of Business-to-Business (B2B) e-commerce.
133. For a more detailed discussion of electronic signatures as such the reader is directed to Chapter 2 of Part III of the present work (Electronic Signatures).

126. Other important topics relevant to electronic contracting are Consumer Protection,[134] a 'Cooling-off Period',[135] spam and unsolicited goods,[136] electronic payment systems (such as PayPal)[137] and really exciting new developments such as 'smart contracts' and 'blockchain' and the development of new means of payment (including cryptocurrencies such as Bitcoin). Whereas most of the older concepts should be familiar to readers of the present work, the latest developments do merit special discussion.

127. The development of blockchain technology has spurred developments such as the creation of cryptocurrencies, with Bitcoin and Ethereum being examples of the latter. According to expert opinion a blockchain in its simplest form may be described as 'open, public, decentralised ledger that records transactions between two parties in a permanent manner' created by a multitude of participants.[138] This technology is used mostly in cryptocurrency jurisdictions. 'Whereas Bitcoin tracks the ownership of a digital currency, Ethereum provides a means of running the programming code of any decentralised application.'[139]

128. Smart contracts are also dealt with in Chapter 6 of *ICT Law* where it is shown how many diverging views exist on this topic.[140] However, it has been defined as 'computer code that is designed automatically to execute contractual duties upon the occurrence of a trigger event'.[141] This raises the slightly intimidating spectre of an electronic agent deciding to contract, negotiating the terms thereof, concluding such agreement and finally, even fulfilling it. For the time being, however, it seems that smart contracts will remain a blend between computer code and natural language.[142]

134. *Supra* 214ff but also dealt with under a separate heading in the present work (Chapter 6 of Part III dealing with Online Transactions).
135. *Supra* 224ff.
136. *Supra* 226ff.
137. *Supra* 229ff.
138. See Van der Merwe et al., *ICT Law* (2022) Chapter 6 188ff. See the sources in n 148 and especially Eiselen 2019 *THRHR* 634.
139. *Supra* 189ff.
140. *Supra* 186ff.
141. *Supra* 186 n136 citing sources such as Van Huyssteen et al *Contract: General Principles* (2020) 23 as well as Erlank and Ramokanate 2016 *Merc LJ* 204-5.
142. *Supra* 187.

Chapter 2. Electronic Signatures (Including Trust Services and Online Financial Services)

129. Section 13 of the ECT Act is simply entitled 'Signature' and subsection 13(1) provides as follows:

> (1) Where the signature of a person is required by law and such law does not specify the type of signature, that requirement in relation to a data message is met only if an advanced electronic signature is used.

130. Subsection 13(2) provides as follows:

> (2) Subject to subsection (1) an electronic signature is not without legal force and effect merely on the grounds that it is in electronic form.

131. We have already referred in the previous section to an 'advanced electronic signature' and to an ordinary 'electronic signature'. The latter is an electronic signature, defined by section 1 of the ECT Act as 'data generated, sent, received or stored by electronic means' and including voice under certain circumstance as well as 'a stored record'.

132. In order to become 'advanced', the signature has to comply with the provisions of section 38(1) that focus on being uniquely linked to the user, being capable of identifying the user, being created by means which can be kept under his or her sole control, being linked to the message which is being 'signed' in such a way that later changes will be detectable, and being based on an (original) face-to-face identification of the user.

133. Practically, this means that the signatory is no longer using a pen to attach a so-called wet signature (because it uses ink) to the bottom of the page, but is probably first making a 'hash total' (counting the exact number of bits and bytes in the electronic document) and adding some extra bits and bytes (his signature). He would add the latter by means of a private 'key', which can be kept under the sole control of the user and would also identify him or her. The key should only be issued to the user upon personal application and after face-to-face identification. Because the message now carries metadata which informs the recipient computer exactly how many bits and bytes he or she should be receiving, any changes during transmission should be immediately detectable.[143]

134. Subsection 13(3) sets out the following criterion with regard to electronic signatures:

---

143. *See* Part I, Ch. 8 *supra* on the cryptography role players involved in this process.

(3) Where an electronic signature is required by the parties to an electronic transaction and the parties have not agreed on the type of electronic signature to be used, that requirement is met in relation to a data message if –

a method is used to identify the person and to indicate the person's approval of the information communicated; and
having regard to all the relevant circumstances at the time the method was used, the method was as reliable as was appropriate for the purposes for which the information was communicated.

135. The above-mentioned legislative section focuses on the functional equivalents conveyed by the traditional 'wet signature'. These are the elements of identification (or 'authentication' in a slightly wider sense), non-repudiability (once a person has given his or her approval he or she cannot again retract it) and reliability. If the proper equipment is used, the electronic signature should perform these functions as well, or even better, when compared to the traditional 'wet' signature.

136. Subsection 13(4) provides the following:

(4) Where an advanced electronic signature has been used, such signature is regarded as being a valid electronic signature and to have been applied properly, unless the contrary is proved.

137. This subsection quoted in the previous paragraph carries a lot of dynamite. It places the burden of proof onto the person who alleges that the advanced electronic signature had some defect to prove the allegation. If, after all, is said and done, the court still entertains doubt as to the real situation, it will decide against the party that bore the burden of proof. In other words, any party using an advanced electronic signature will always get the benefit of the doubt.

138. Subsection 13(5) simply provides that an electronic signature and data message are not the only means by which a person's intent or other statement may be inferred.

139. As we have seen with the evidential sections, 'authentication' is of the utmost importance in order for the court to accept electronic documents[144] as evidence and to attach the proper weight to these instruments of proof. If one wants the considerable procedural advantages of an 'advanced' electronic signature, one needs to deal with cryptography and the specialized role players in this regard.

144. Termed 'data messages' by the ECT Act.

140. The ECT Act creates a number of statutory bodies to assist with these requirements. In the first place, the Act[145] defines an 'authentication service provider' as follows: '(A) person whose authentication products or services have been accredited by the Accreditation Authority under section 37 or recognized under section 40.'

141. This brings the 'Accreditation Authority' into play. This is not defined in the definition section of the ECT Act, but in Chapter VI, which deals with 'authentication service providers'. As seen from the previous paragraph, this is a class of people who are dependent on the Accreditation Authority for their very existence. The Accreditation Authority turns out to be none other than the Director General of the DOC[146] who may also, after consultation with the minister, appoint employees of that department as 'Deputy Accreditation Authorities and Officers'.[147]

142. The process of 'accreditation' itself is also statutorily defined as 'recognition of an authentication product or service by the Accreditation Authority'.[148] This effectively means that the Director General of the DOC has the final say on the entire subject of 'accreditation' and, as a result thereof, also on the subject of 'authentication'. Fortunately, the criteria for accreditation are spelt out in the Act.[149]

143. The criteria for an 'electronic signature' are set out as follows: First, the Accreditation Authority has to be satisfied that the electronic signature to which the authentication products or services relate:[150]

(1) is uniquely linked to the user;
(2) is capable of identifying that user;
(3) is created using means that can be maintained under the sole control of that user;
(4) will be linked to the data or data message to which it relates in such a manner that any subsequent change of the data or data message is detectable;
(5) is based on the face-to-face identification of the user'.

144. In coming to a final finding on the long-term reliability of an authentication service provider, the Accreditation Authority will have regard to the following factors:[151]

(a) its financial and human resources, including its assets;
(b) the quality of its hardware and software systems;
(c) its procedures for processing products or services;

---

145. In s. 1, the definition section.
146. Department of Communications. *See* s. 34(1) of the ECT Act.
147. Section 34(2) of the ECT Act.
148. Section 33 of the ECT Act.
149. Section 38 of the Act.
150. Section 38(1).
151. Section 38(2).

(d) the availability of information to third parties relying on the authentication product or service;
(e) the regularity and extent of audits by an independent body;
(f) the factors referred to in subsection (4), where the products and services are rendered by a certification service provider; and
(g) any other relevant factor which may be prescribed.

145. The criteria to which the hardware and software systems mentioned above have to live up[152] to are that they must:

(a) be reasonably secure from intrusion and misuse;
(b) provide a reasonable level of availability, reliability and correct operation;
(c) be reasonably suited to performing their intended functions; and
(d) adhere to generally accepted security procedures.

146. After this, when the products or services are provided by a certification service provider, the accreditation may also stipulate:

(a) the technical and other requirements which certificates must meet;
(b) the requirements for issuing certificates;
(c) the requirements for certification practice statements;
(d) the responsibilities of the certification service provider;
(e) the liability of the certification service provider;
(f) the records to be kept and the manner in which[153] and length of time for which they must be kept;
(g) requirements as to adequate certificate suspension and revocation procedures;
(h) requirements as to adequate notification procedures relating to certificate suspension and revocation.

147. Finally, one comes to the central figure as far as the whole process is concerned, the cryptography service provider. This cryptography service provider mentioned in section 81(1)(b) is not defined in the Act, but section 1 does define 'cryptography service' as follows:

> any service which is provided to a sender or a recipient of a data message or to anyone storing a data message, and which is designed to facilitate the use of cryptographic techniques for the purpose of ensuring –
>
> > that such data or data message can be accessed or can be put into an intelligible form only by certain persons;
> > that the authenticity or integrity of such data or data message is capable of being ascertained;
> > the integrity of the data or data message;

152. Section 38(3).
153. One would think that this is the ideal place to determine whether digital storage would be adequate, or whether some form of 'hard copy' should be kept.

or that the source of the data or data message can be correctly ascertained.

148. From the above, it is clear that cryptography may play a major role with regard to the 'chain of evidence' when used with regard to data, data messages, or information. Any team investigating a crime scene would, therefore, do well to also include a cryptography expert in their midst. The cryptography service providers will make their money from participating in e-commerce, however, and helping to guarantee those services.[154]

Administering all these multifarious activities seems like a tall order for a government department that also has to run the post office, radio and television services, telecommunications in general, and similar activities. For this reason, criticism of these provisions has not been long in coming. According to *Cyberlaw @SA II*[155] these types of activities are:

> already satisfactorily performed by technically sophisticated organisations in the *private*[156] sector, both in South Africa and worldwide. These organizations have earned the necessary trust from the communities they serve. Considering that the cost of establishing the administrative capacity to adequately perform this function will be high, and that the benefits the Department of Communications envisions are unlikely, the value of this chapter is doubtful.

149. This criticism does have some merit, particularly since the Director General, who had been the moving spirit behind the legislation itself, has since moved on to the private sector himself. Nonetheless, Africa is a continent that takes much easier to state socialism than to individualistic capitalism, and the present framework might be more workable in the long run for South Africa and its African neighbours. The question remains, however, if this will be acceptable to its European and American trading partners, who are very suspicious of state involvement in the business of making money, which is really what e-commerce is all about. Barring involvement by the United Nations, however, the state might still be the best 'referee' in overseeing hard competition between participants in the game of e-commerce.[157]

150. In the end, the author of the criticism voiced in the last quotation concedes that, practically, the South African requirements for advanced digital signatures are not that different from those set by our European counterparts.[158]

---

154. *See also* Part I Chapter 1 supra on the Regulation of Cryptography and the providers thereof.
155. Buys (ed.), *Cyberlaw@SA* II (2004) at 124–125. These comments have not been repeated in *Cyberlaw@SA III* (2012) Snail & Papadopoulos (eds).
156. My own emphasis.
157. Barring corruption, which unfortunately is still too prevalent in Africa.
158. Buys (ed.), *Cyberlaw@SA II* (2004) at 133.

151. One of the potentially valuable developments in this regard has been the publication of regulations[159] on the functions of the Accreditation Authority and its relation to authentication service providers, as well as to certification service providers. Although mostly formal in nature, it is clear that the intention is to keep to international standards such as X 509v3 as far as authentication is concerned and to ISO/IEC 17799 as far as security is concerned. The latter standard has been adopted by the South African Bureau for Standards (SABS) as SABS 17799.

152. Unfortunately, the forensic testing of the practical application of these regulations or standards has not taken place very often. Mention will later again be made of the case of *S v. Ndiki*[160] when the events in question took place before the ECT Act[161] had come into operation, but the trial was held after the Act came into operation. Van Zyl J. found that this point did not have to be decided in order to reach a conclusion, because the matter was covered by existing law. A series of documents were involved, and the court felt that these could be classified into two groups. The first group contained witnesses' statements of fact, which had been stored on a computer. The court decided that the computer being used as a storage medium did not influence the inherently hearsay nature of these statements. In the end, the hearsay statements were admitted into evidence within the discretion of the court. The second group of documents had been created by the computer without direct human intervention. Because these could be categorized as the product of the machine, they were admitted as real evidence.

153. The above case may be placed next to *Ndlovu v. Minister of Correctional Services and Another*[162] when the defence argued that a two-page computer printout was not admissible as evidence because it was not the original document. This argument was rejected on technical grounds, but the court held obiter that section 15 of the ECT Act did not supersede the hearsay provisions contained in the Law of Evidence Amendment Act, Act 45 of 1988.

154. Trust services have an important role to play in providing a guarantee (in the form of a certificate) for the authenticity of a specific electronic signature. In South Africa, the Post Office was supposed to have played a major role in this regard, but they have not lived up to expectations. By contrast, the private firm Lawtrust[163] provides reliable service with regard to electronic signing solutions, SSL[164] certificates and other 'paperless initiatives'.

---

159. Notice 1573 of 2004 published in GG 26602 of 31 Jul. 2004.
160. 2007 [2] All SA 185 (Ck) and *see ICT Law* (2022) by Van der Merwe et al., 138ff. *See also* the section on Criminal Law infra (Part VI).
161. Act 25 of 2002.
162. [2006] 4 All SA 165 (W).
163. See *lawtrust.co.za* in this regard.
164. Secure Sockets Layer.

155. Most business is done remotely nowadays by means of e-mail, web pages or even on the 'Zoom' and 'Teams' forums. Online financial services are also ubiquitous, and everyone is banking by means of the Internet or even on their cell phones. This has led to a drastic diminution in 'walk-in' branches of the main South African banks.

Chapter 3. Law of Evidence in the Digital Environment (Including Rules Regarding Electronic Archiving)

§1. Background

156. As mentioned earlier, the law of evidence is part of an adjective or procedural law. Whereas another branch of adjective law, the law of criminal procedure (to be dealt with in Part VI *infra*), is responsible for the collection of possible relevant evidence, the law of evidence determines the admissibility and weight thereof. Because of this historical legacy, the law of evidence is based mostly on English as well as locally developed law. Roman-Dutch law has little or no influence in this area.

157. The coming of the computer has thrown the law of evidence into confusion. Traditionally, the law of evidence dealt with viva voce evidence (oral evidence by a witness actually testifying in court), real evidence (physical objects such as a knife as murder weapon), and documentary evidence (literally pieces of paper). The law of evidence is yet undecided whether to put electronic computer-generated evidence into the category of real evidence or into the category of documentary evidence. A third option might be to declare it to be a sui generis (of its own unique kind) type of evidence, for which new principles have to be developed.

158. One of the most valuable pointers as to the weight to be accorded to each piece of evidence is the use of cross-examination. After a witness has concluded giving his or her viva voce evidence, he or she may then be cross-examined by the opposing party of the latter's legal counsel. Even though one humorist has described this procedure as 'examining the witness crossly', it is really a much more skilful procedure. Basically, it consists of pointing out vagueness and internal contradictions in testimony to the witness and demanding an explanation or a resolution of these. It is also important to confront the witness with possible bias and to put the view of the opposing side (as persuasively as possible) before the witness to accept or deny. In practice, witnesses are sometimes reduced to tears by this gruelling experience (although the court should protect witnesses against real abuse) and sometimes admit that their testimony has not been truthful.

159. With regard to real evidence, a witness has to give supporting evidence in order to place the object into perspective, for instance, where the blood-stained knife was found and how it was taken care of until brought before the court (the 'chain of evidence' mentioned above). Some courts are of the opinion that 'products of modern technology' should be treated as real evidence. In two South African cases, *S v. Mpumlo* [165] and *S v. Baleka* (1),[166] it was decided that video and audio tapes should be treated as real evidence (being a 'thing'). However, in *S v. Singh* [167]

165. 1986 (3) SA 485 (E).
166. 1986 (4) SA 192 (T).
167. 1975 (1) SA 330 (N).

and *S v. Ramgobin*,[168] it was decided that the output of these machines was sufficiently close to documents to treat these tapes as documentary evidence.

160. One of the disadvantages of documentary evidence is that the person making a statement on paper cannot be cross-examined to test the weight and validity of that statement (unless he or she happens to be physically present in the court). If the person is physically present to give evidence, it would obviate the need for documentary evidence in the first place.

161. In whatever category one puts computer-based evidence, it is very likely that the person having made a statement by means of this medium would probably not be present in court to be cross-examined on the facts contained in this statement.

§2. The Computer Evidence Act[169]

162. This piece of legislation arose directly from a court case. In *Narlis v. South African Bank of Athens*,[170] the court was confronted with a computer printout as potential evidence and found that this was not admissible as evidence according to the then state of the law. The actual words used by the judge were: 'Well, a computer, perhaps fortunately, is not a person.'

163. The result of the case described in the previous paragraph led to a clamour for law reform from almost every organization that had been using computers to store their information. The Clearing Bankers' Association instructed a South African judge, Justice Didcott, to prepare a report and draft bill on their behalf. This was presented to the South African Law Commission (SALC),[171] who handed their own report and recommendations to the Minister of Justice.

164. The resulting Act assumed that the output from a computer would be documentary evidence (probably because the electronic data were printed out on paper as hard copy). This Act was confined to civil cases, probably because unrepresented accused would not be able to give an informed consent to, or be able to oppose effectively, computer evidence put in against them. Another interesting point was that civil cases provided for the discovery and inspection of all documentary evidence before the trial started, whereas criminal prosecutions did not do so (except in a rudimentary form). Finally, the consequences of a criminal prosecution might be far more serious to the individual, because his or her liberty might be at stake.

---

168. 1986 (4) SA 117 (N).
169. Act 57 of 1983.
170. 1976 (2) SA 573 (A).
171. A body which is responsible for repealing old, and initiating new legislation in South Africa.

165. The Act was criticized almost universally by academics and almost entirely ignored by practice. It, therefore, rapidly became a dead letter, and it seemed obvious that new (and better) legislation was needed. The main reason for the failure of this act, in my opinion, is that it still operated in terms of paper printouts, instead of addressing the dynamic and changeable nature of information. It has been expressly repealed by legislation discussed under the next heading.

§3. Evidential Aspects of the ECT Act

I. Background

166. This piece of legislation has also undergone a long gestation process. It was preceded by a Green Paper on Electronic Commerce, which made certain recommendations towards new legislation.[172] Simultaneously the SALC also produced a report and recommendations with regard to computer crime.[173] This was followed by the work of a Task Team of the DOC, which incorporated the work done by the other organizations.

167. This section will deal first with the narrowly evidential provisions of the ECT Act and will then[174] endeavour to show how these link in with the new bodies created by that act, particularly in connection with cryptography.

II. Evidential Provisions of the ECT Act

168. Chapter III of the ECT Act deals with 'Facilitating Electronic Transactions' and sections 11–20 deal specifically with 'Legal Requirements for Data Messages' – in other words, the requirements before they would be admitted as evidence in court proceedings.

169. Section 11 is entitled 'Legal Recognition of Data Messages' and provides the following in that regard:

(1) Information is not without legal force and effect merely on the grounds that it is wholly or partly in the form of a data message.
(2) Information is not without legal force and effect merely on the grounds that is not contained in the data message purporting to give rise to such legal force and effect but is merely referred to in such data message.
(3) Information incorporated into an agreement and that is not in the public domain is regarded as having been incorporated into a data message if such information is – referred to in a way in which a reasonable person would have noticed the reference thereto and incorporation thereof; and accessible

172. Act 25 of 2002.
173. *See* paras 438–439 and 466.
174. *See* in this regard also Part I, Ch. 8 *supra*.

in a form in which it may be read, stored and retrieved by the other party, whether electronically or as a computer printout as long as such information is reasonably capable of being reduced to electronic form by the party incorporating it.

170. The section described in the previous paragraph is the basic passport for data messages to be admitted into court as evidence, whether in criminal or civil cases. (The ECT Act also repealed the whole of the old Computer Evidence Act.)[175] Section 11 also deals with 'incorporation by reference' – a valuable provision in a world where the Internet is held together by hyperlinks (a highlighted word in a page of electronic text, which when clicked upon, takes one to a different page of electronic text). This would also enable one to have a single 'electronic signpost' at the end of an e-mail message, for instance, redirecting one to a more copious set of terms and conditions which apply to that particular message. According to section 11, the cross-referenced text is part of the conditions for the admissibility in evidence of the main document, provided that the cross-reference text is accessible and retrievable by the other party.

Section 12 of the ECT Act is simply entitled 'Writing' and provides the following in that regard:

> A requirement in law that a document or form must be in writing is met if the document or information is – in the form of a data message; and accessible in a manner usable for subsequent reference.

171. By emphasizing the aspect of 'writing', it is clear that the ECT Act has considered the traditional requirements for documentary evidence, for example, that such evidence has to be in writing. Instead, the new Act has focused on the underlying value, namely that the evidence has to be accessible for further reference. This requirement might not be without its problems since the hardware needed to retrieve such data changed at a dizzying speed. Would the custodian of certain electronic documents formatted and stored on an Apple II computer in 1985, therefore, need to keep an Apple machine in working order to be able to retrieve the data in future?

172. A better solution might be to do regular 'migration' of the data, from soon-to-be-obsolete hardware to more recent technology. However, this might have considerable cost implications.

173. A document stored or presented in electronic format would, therefore, comply with the new requirements of the law of evidence. As a practical example, one thinks of an offer to sell or buy immovable property, which according to statute, needs to be in 'writing'. According to the ECT Act, this 'written' offer would be adequate. Be careful, though, in that specific legislation might override the more general provision of the ECT Act in this regard.

175. Act 57 of 1983.

174. Subsection 13(1) of the ECT Act deals with electronic signatures and provides that where a signature is required 'by law' and that law does not further specify the type of signature, this requirement shall only be met if an advanced electronic signature had been used. Subject to this, subsection 13(2) specifies that an electronic signature shall not be without force and effect, merely because it is in electronic form. Unfortunately, clause 13 as a whole does not make it sufficiently clear what the position of a signature 'by law' would be – whether the signature should be 'by law' in terms of a statute, or whether the common law would also qualify. Where a valid advanced electronic signature has been used, this places an evidentiary burden on a party wishing to dispute the authenticity of this signature.[176] *See* further in this regard Chapter III of the ECT Act.

175. Section 14 of the ECT Act is entitled 'Original' and subsection 14(1) has the following to say:

(1) Where a law requires information to be presented or retained in its original form, that requirement is met by a data message if – the integrity of the information from the time when it was first generated in its final form as a data message or otherwise has passed assessment in terms of subsection (2); and that information is capable of being displayed or produced to the person to whom it is to be presented.
(2) For the purposes of subsection 1 the integrity must be assessed – by considering whether the information has remained complete and unaltered except for the addition of any endorsement and any change which arises in the normal course of communication, storage and display; in the light of the purpose for which the information was generated; and having regard to all other relevant circumstances.

This section is purely to deal with the requirement, in documentary evidence, that the original of any paper document always has to be presented to the court in evidence.

176. The reason for this is quite straightforward. If the court has the original document before it to scrutinize, it might be able to discern any alterations, erasures, etc., that would tend to make the document less reliable. In fact, the forensics department of the SAPS should be able to perform tests on the document, which would indicate the age of the paper, the weight on the pen when writing or performing a signature, which of two lines crossing each other had been made first, etc.

177. Section 15 of the ECT Act deals with the 'Admissibility and Evidential Weight of Data Messages' and subsection 15(1) reads as follows:

(1) In any legal proceedings, the rules of evidence must not be applied so as to deny the possibility of a data message, in evidence –

176. *See* ss. 13(4) of the Act.

on the mere grounds that it is constituted by a data message; or
if it is the best evidence that the person adducing it could reasonably be expected to obtain, on the ground that is not in its original form.

178. This specific clause has already been used in an (as-yet unreported) divorce matter before the Cape Supreme Court to admit printed copies of e-mail messages. Of course, admissibility is only the first stage of the proceedings; the court would later on have to decide how much weight is to be awarded to the admitted evidence. This is addressed in paragraphs 182–184 below.

179. The 'best evidence' rule is part of our heritage from the British law of evidence. If the original document, which is normally required as evidence as we have seen above, is not available or has been lost or destroyed, the court might admit the best alternative as the 'best evidence' under the circumstances.

180. Subsections 15(2) and (3) read as follows:

(2) Information in the form of a data message must be given due evidential weight.
(3) In assessing the evidential weight of a data message, regard must be had to – the reliability of the manner in which the data message was generated, stored or communicated;
 (3) the reliability of the manner in which the integrity of the data message was maintained;
 (4) the manner in which its originator was identified; and
 (5) any other relevant factor.

181. Subsection 15(2) is not very helpful with its vague criterion of 'due evidential weight', but at least makes it clear that one cannot simply ignore important evidence, simply because it is not in hard copy format, but originated from an electronic data message.

182. Subsection 15(3) does set out some valuable guidelines that a court (as well as legal counsel on both sides) might follow in arguing the evidential weight of a data message. Subsection 15(3)(a) deals with the 'chain of evidence' which has previously been mentioned in this document.

183. Subsection 15(3)(b) deals with the integrity or 'wholeness' of the particular data message. Not one bit or byte should be missing from the checksum that the computer has initially made of the data contained in the data message. The only way in which this may be done reliably would be to encrypt the data. However, because of the tombstone programs (explained in paragraph 441), one should also make a hard copy printout of the data message before encrypting it.

184. Subsection 15(3)(c) deals with the very important factor of the identification of the original author of the data message. Proving that something comes from someone specifically is the crucial factor of authentication. In fact, authorship and integrity should both be present before a document can be called 'authentic', which means that the document 'does not tell a lie about itself'.

185. The 'any other relevant factor' mentioned by subsection 15(3)(d) is an open variable that acts as a kind of 'dragnet clause' to prevent this portion of the legislation from being overtaken by technological developments.

186. Subsection 15(4) reads as follows:

> (4) A data message made by a person in the ordinary course of business, or a copy or printout of or an extract from such data message certified to be correct by an officer in the service of such person, is on its mere production in any civil, criminal, or disciplinary proceedings under any law, the rules of a self-regulatory organization or any other law or the common-law, admissible in evidence against any person and rebuttable proof of the facts contained in such record, copy, printout or extract.

187. Subsection 15(4) constitutes the so-called shop-book exception that South Africa has inherited from British law. Because busy tradesmen do not have the time to spend on the special care of the thousands of transactions which speed through their data systems every day, a data message which passes through 'in the ordinary course' of business is presumed to be admissible in evidence. Not only is the evidence admissible, but it provides a rebuttable presumption in favour of the correctness of the data message. This means that the party who wishes to allege that the data message is incorrect will have to bear the onus of proof in that regard. In a civil case, this would require proof 'on a preponderance of probabilities', but in criminal cases, the criterion is even higher. The prosecution in a criminal matter has to prove all facts 'beyond reasonable doubt'.

188. It is also of interest that this subsection takes the trouble of enumerating the different types of proceedings where the exception will find application and mentions the common law specifically. As has been mentioned,[177] the common law for the South African Law of Evidence is the British law, or rather 'the law in force on 30 May 1961'.

189. In general, section 15 may be seen as the heart of not only the evidential part but of the whole ECT Act. At a single stroke, it (satisfyingly) addresses all the arguments which lawyers (including the author) have been making for many years regarding the admissibility and weight of documents which originate from a computer.

190. Section 16 of the ECT Act deals with 'Retention' (of documentary evidence) and reads as follows:

177. *See* para. 465 *supra*.

(1) Where a law requires information to be retained, that requirement is met by retaining such information in the form of a data message, if –

the information contained in the data message is accessible so as to be usable for subsequent reference;
the data message is in the format in which it was generated, sent or received, or in a format which can be demonstrated to represent accurately the information generated, sent or received; and
the origin and destination of that data message and the date and time it was sent or received can be determined.

(2) The obligation to retain information as contemplated in subsection (1) does not extend to any information the sole purpose of which is to enable the message to be sent or received.

191. A number of statutes impose an obligation on certain persons and legal persons to preserve important documents for various time periods. The argument behind this doctrine of the 'retention of documents' is that if anything goes wrong, those documents might be needed as proof in future court or quasi-judicial proceedings.

192. Some of these acts are (and were): the Companies Act,[178] the Stamp Duties Act,[179] the Income Tax Act,[180] the Customs and Excise Act,[181] the Basic Conditions of Employment Act,[182] the Compensation for Occupational Injuries and Diseases Act,[183] the Machinery and Occupational Safety Act[184] (specifically in the regulations), the Insolvency Act,[185] and the Value Added Tax (VAT) Act.[186] This list is by no means exhaustive.

193. The merit of section 16 is that the retention of records in the form of electronic messages is now allowed. This point has been a bone of contention among lawyers for many years. The specific requirements of the section have been discussed already, except for subsection 16(2). The latter determines that even though the origin and destination and date and time of the message need to be preserved, other routing information or 'metadata' does not need to be retained in order to be able to use the law as set out in subsection 16(1).

194. Section 17 deals with the 'Production of document or information'. Subsection 17(1) reads as follows:

178. Act 71 of 2008.
179. Act 77 of 1968 (abolished with effect from midnight on 31 Mar. 2009).
180. Act 58 of 1962.
181. Act 91 of 1964.
182. Act 75 of 1997.
183. Act 130 of 1993.
184. Act 6 of 1983.
185. Act 24 of 1936.
186. Act 89 of 1991.

(1) Subject to sec. 28, where a law requires a person to produce a document or information, that requirement is met if the person produces, by means of a data message, an electronic form of that document or information, and if – considering all the relevant circumstances at the time that the data message was sent, the method of generating the electronic form of that document provided a reliable means of assuring the maintenance of the integrity of the information contained in that document; and at the time the data message was sent, it was reasonable to expect that the information contained therein would be readily accessible so as to be usable for subsequent reference.

195. The 'production' of a document to court is mostly used in civil procedure but may also turn up in criminal proceedings. Readers should by now be familiar with phrases such as 'reliable' and 'integrity' and the question of 'accessibility for subsequent reference'.

196. Subsection 17(2) introduces a new concept, however, and reads as follows:

(2) For the purposes of subsection (1), the integrity of the information contained in a document is maintained if the information has remained complete and unaltered, except for – the addition of any endorsement; or any immaterial change, which arises in the normal course of communication, storage or display.

197. In this case, we are again dealing with 'metadata', except for one very important matter. An endorsement is almost the same as a 'signature', which was discussed above. Even though the present subsection allows endorsement by implication, such endorsement would still have to comply with the requirements of an electronic signature, as set out in section 13 of the Act.

198. Subsection 18 deals with 'Notarization, acknowledgment, and certification' and reads as follows:

(1) Where a law requires a signature, statement or document to be notarized, acknowledged, verified or made under oath, that requirement is met if the advanced electronic signature of the person authorized to perform those acts is attached to, incorporated in or logically associated with the electronic signature or data message;
(2) Where a law requires of, or permits a person to provide a certified copy of a document and the document exists in electronic form, that requirement is met if the person provides a printout certified to be a true reproduction of the document or information;
(3) Where a law requires or permits a person to provide a certified copy of a document and the document exists in paper or other physical form, that requirement is met if an electronic copy of the document is certified to be a true copy thereof and the certificate is confirmed by the use of an advanced electronic signature.

199. Subsection 18(1) deals with those functions carried out by men and women called 'sworn notaries and conveyancers'. We are not particularly concerned with the conveyancing side of things, but what exactly is the 'notary' that we often see on the shop windows and business cards of lawyers? Basically, a notary is a type of 'super witness' who will co-sign a document with the original signatory, store the document away safely and if any doubt should ever arise as to the authenticity of the document, the notary will be able to testify that the document is genuine.

200. Subsections 18(2) and (3) deal with the portability of data between electronic and hard copies of the same document. An interesting requirement is that an advanced electronic signature (discussed under section 13 and at other relevant places) be used to place the integrity of the data (as well as the signatory) above suspicion.

201. Section 19 deals with 'Other requirements' and subsection 19(1) has this to say on the first of the 'other requirements':

> (1) A requirement in law for multiple copies of a document to be submitted to a single addressee at the same time is satisfied by the submission of a single data message that is capable of being reproduced by that addressee.

202. This would seem to be a common-sense clause that trades on the great benefit of having digital copies – they can be reproduced almost indefinitely.

203. Subsection 19(2) reads as follows:

> (2) An expression in a law, whether used as a noun or verb, including the terms 'document', 'record', 'file', 'submit', 'lodge', 'deliver', 'issue', 'publish', 'write in', 'print' or words or expressions of similar effect, must be interpreted so as to include or permit such form, format, or action in relation to a data message unless otherwise provided for in this Act.

204. From the words used in this subsection, it appears that computer-generated evidence will fall squarely into the category of documentary evidence. The above terms all relate to actions, which used to be performed with regard to paper documents. It is to be welcomed that data messages will now be able to fulfil the same functions. This takes our law away from the focus on printouts, which categorized the old Computer Evidence Act.[187]

205. Subsection 19(3) runs as follows:

> (3) Where a seal is required to be affixed to a document and such law does not prescribe the method or form by which such document may be sealed by electronic means, that requirement is met if the document indicates that it

187. Act 57 of 1983.

is required to be under seal and it includes the advanced electronic signature of the person by whom it is required to be sealed.

206. As was mentioned in the previous paragraph, the equivalent of sealing may now be carried out with an electronic signature as part of an electronic document. The guarantees given by using an advanced electronic signature fulfil the same function as the unbroken seal did with hard copy documents.

207. Subsection 19(4) contains the following text:

> (4) Where the law requires or permits a person to send a document or information by registered or certified post or similar service, that requirement is met if an electronic copy of the document or information is sent to the South African Post Office Limited, registered by the said Post Office and sent by the Post Office to the electronic address provided by the sender.

208. The requirement postulated in the previous paragraph was truly an interesting innovation. It does impose responsibility on the post office to obtain the necessary technical equipment to 'register' such document of information and to ensure the integrity of its data in transmission. In all probability, the post office would need to make use of encryption techniques to bring the security of the message at least up to the standards provided by an advanced electronic signature. Unfortunately, as has been stated before, the South African Post Office no longer seems able to carry out such specialized functions.

209. Section 20 deals with 'Automated Transactions' and describes the procedure as follows:

> In an automated transaction –
>
> > an agreement may be formed where an electronic agent performs an action required by law for agreement formation;
> > an agreement may be formed where all parties to a transaction or either one of them uses an electronic agent;

210. A contractor using an electronic agent to form an agreement is, subject to paragraph (d), presumed to be bound by the terms of that agreement irrespective of whether that person reviewed the actions of the electronic agent or the terms of the agreement;

211. A party interacting with an electronic agent to form an agreement is not bound by the terms of the agreement unless those terms were capable of being reviewed by a natural person representing that party prior to the agreement formation; no agreement is formed where a natural person interacts directly with the electronic agent of another person and has made a material error during the creation of that message and:

(i) the electronic agent did not provide that person with an opportunity to prevent or correct the error;
(ii) that person notifies the other person of the error as soon as practicable after that person has learned of it;
(iii) that person takes reasonable steps, including steps that conform to the other person's instructions to return any performance received, or if instructed to do so, to destroy that performance;
(iv) that person has not used or received any material benefit or value from the performance received by the other person.

212. The above-mentioned piece of legislation introduces the interesting technical (and legal) concept of an 'electronic agent'. This is of course nothing other than a computer program, pre-programmed with some artificial intelligence to check whether all the technicalities and formalities of an agreement have been complied with.

213. It is also interesting to note that as long as the dealings by the electronic agent were capable of being reviewed by a person, it is unimportant that the person did not actually take the trouble to do so. This is to avoid wilful neglect by the one party to actually review the process if he or she wishes to sabotage the whole agreement.

214. A number of sensible error-correcting principles are also built into this section. In a penetrating work by the American author Lawrence Lessig, called *Code*, the point is made that more and more legal work will be taken over by the architecture of hardware and software, because the outcome is much more certain than when left to the tender mercies of lawyers.

Chapter 4. Consumer Protection of the Users of Electronic Services (Online Sales and Services)

§1. Introduction

215. This field may be seen as a late bloomer in South African law, perhaps because it has never really been developed in the common law of South Africa, the Roman-Dutch law. It is, therefore, interesting that such a new field as computer law is playing a pioneering role in making decent consumer protection part of the South African legal scene. Buys, in *Cyberlaw@SA,*[188] actually speculates whether it might not be unconstitutional 'to provide online consumers with more rights and protections than offline consumers'. He provides his own answer[189] by a realization that online consumers have very little of the additional guarantees of quality and trust which face-to-face contact with customers bring. A specialized Consumer Protection Act[190] has entered upon the South African legal scene and although wide enough to embrace computer issues it was felt that the relevant portions of the ECT Act were specialized enough to justify the continued existence of the latter Act. The provisions of the two Act, therefore, need to be considered jointly when dealing with this type of issue.[191]

§2. Consumer Protection in Terms of the ECT Act

216. The ECT Act[192] has introduced, among many other innovations, the concept of 'protection during electronic transactions' to the South African consumer. These provisions are contained in Chapter 7 of the ECT Act and the protection they provide is limited to 'electronic transactions',[193] although there are a number of additional exclusions.[194] These relate, for instance, to financial services, auctions, goods intended for everyday consumption, where selling price is dependent on fluctuations in financial markets which cannot be controlled by the supplier, where the goods are made to the customer's specifications[195] or are clearly personalized, where audio and video recordings of computer software have been unsealed by the consumer, for the sale of newspapers and other reading matter, for the provision of gaming and lottery services, or for the provision of accommodation or catering or similar services.

217. A supplier furthermore has to provide the consumer with certain information on the website where the goods are offered,[196] with an opportunity to review

188. Van Schaiks (2004), at 139-140; *see also* Van der Merwe et al *ICT Law* (2022) 214ff.
189. Correctly, in the present author's opinion.
190. Act 68 of 2008.
191. *See* Van der Merwe et al., *supra* 216.
192. Act 25 of 2002. *See* too in general, Van der Merwe et al., *supra* 215ff.
193. Section 42(1) of the Act. 'Electronic transactions' are left strangely undefined in the act.
194. Section 42(2).
195. A bespoke, tailor-made suit would be a good example.
196. Section 43(1).

the transaction or withdraw from it and to cancel such transaction within fourteen days of receiving the goods.[197] A 'consumer' is defined as 'any natural person who enters or intends entering into an electronic transaction with a supplier as the end user of the goods or services offered by that supplier'.[198]

218. The Act further provides such niceties as a compulsory cooling-off period[199] as well as for certain other options with regard to unsolicited goods, services, or communications.[200] The so-called cooling-off relates to giving a consumer, who may have been overwhelmed by the immediate attractions of the product, or by clever salesmanship, an opportunity to reflect coolly on his (or her) purchase and to resign from the contract if it does not survive scrutiny in the cold light of the day. This right may be exercised within seven days after the date of the receipt of the goods, or in the case of services, within seven days after the conclusion of the agreement.[201]

219. The unsolicited goods include communications,[202] and no agreement may be concluded from a lack of response from the receiver of the communications.[203] A person sending such communications after having been notified that they were unwelcome is guilty of an offence and liable to the penalties described in section 89(1) of the ECT Act.[204] This would constitute 'spam' and while it is a good thing that the South African legislature has finally addressed this issue, it may be argued that the method of dealing with spam is not effective. Most spam senders will not reply to e-mails but merely accept requests for termination as a sign that the spam is working. Because they are sending from overseas addresses, it is unlikely that they will be frightened off by the threatened criminal provision.

220. In an analysis of the consumer protection provisions of the act, the authors of the work *ICT Law*[205] differentiate between the scope of the consumer provisions of the Act (rights of consumers, the definition of 'electronic transaction', and statutory exclusions), the informational duties of the web-trader, the transactional duties of the web-trader, a 'cooling-off'-period, the preservation of rights and 'spam'.

---

197. Section 43(2) and (3).
198. Section 1.
199. Section 44.
200. Section 45.
201. Section 44(1)(a) and (b).
202. Which includes spam, of course.
203. Section 45(2).
204. Section 45(3).
205. Van der Merwe et al., *ICT Law* (2022), at 217ff.

§3. Access to Information in the South African Context

221. South Africa enjoys constitutional protection to the polar opposite of the right to privacy, namely the right to have access to information. This right, of course, relates to information that one needs in order to enforce one's constitutional rights.

222. This right to information is contained in section 32 of the South African Constitution.[206] Otherwise, as has been the case with privacy, the South African government was quite quick to pass legislation to give effect to the right of freedom of expression.

223. This has happened in the shape of legislation known by the acronym PROATIA.[207] The object of the act is to facilitate access to information and thereby to give effect to the constitutional right in this regard. It applies to the public and to the private sector. A 'public body' is defined to mean, *inter alia*,: 'any department of state or administration in the national or provincial sphere of government or any municipality in the local sphere of government'[208] and a private body as: 'a natural person, which carries or has carried on any trade, business or profession but only in such capacity, a partnership which carries or has carried on any trade, business or profession or any former existing juristic person but excludes a public body'.

224. In terms of PROATIA, a requester should be given access to any record of a particular body, provided that he (or she) complies with the following conditions:

(1) the record is required for the exercise or protection of any rights;
(2) the requestor complies with the procedural requirements of PROATIA;
(3) access must or may not be refused in terms of one of the mandatory discretionary grounds of refusal, listed in PROATIA.

225. Of course, the body that holds the desired record may refuse access, particularly if the privacy rights of any third party may be involved. However, a number of exceptions are listed[209] in terms of which a record may not be refused, namely:

(1) if the individual concerned has consented in terms of sections 48 and 72 of PROATIA as the case may be;
(2) where information is already publicly available;
(3) where the individual was informed by the body before giving the information that the information would or might be made available to the public;

206. Act 108 of 1996.
207. Act 25 of 2000.
208. Section 1 of Act 25 of 2000.
209. Sections 34(2) and 63(2) with respect to public and private bodies respectively.

(4) where the information relates to the physical or mental health of well-being of an individual who is under the age of 18 or incapable of understanding the nature of the request, and giving access would be in the individual's best interest;
(5) where the information is about a deceased individual and the next of kin is the requester or the request is made with the written consent of the deceased's next of kin.

226. In terms of the Act, the keepers of information have to make manuals available to inform interested parties concerning the procedures to gain access to requested information.

Chapter 5. The Liability of Online Service Providers

227. An interesting innovation in the preliminary drafts of the current Computer Crime Act[210] was a section dealing with the Liability of Online Service Providers. Section 54 would have imposed important reporting obligations on electronic communication service providers in this regard, even leading to possible criminal liability. However, this section was one of those excluded upon the coming into operation of the Computer Crime Act.[211]

228. In the Regulation of the Interception of Communications and Provision of Communications-Related Information Act,[212] section 30 provides that all telecommunication service providers (TSPs), including Internet Service Providers (ISPs), have to store communications-related information for considerable periods of time. In a footnote to this page, Van der Merwe et al.[213] theorizes that this onerous obligation might be to ensure that evidence will be available in the case of later disputes.

229. Online service providers might attract criminal liability with regard to the possession and distribution of pornography but a conviction would only follow if the prosecution can prove *mens rea* on the part of the provider.[214] In South Africa the matter of online pornography is regulated by the Films and Publications Act.[215] Section 27A imposes obligations on service providers provided that any contravention of a criminal prohibition has to be committed 'knowingly'.

230. The question of the liability of online service providers is also relevant when dealing with Defamation and the Infringement of Copyright, but will be dealt with below under the headings of Part VII (Contractual and Non-contractual Liability) and Part IV (Intellectual Rights), respectively.

210. Section 54 of Act 19 of 2020.
211. *See* Van der Merwe et al., *ICT Law* (2022) pp vi and 358.
212. Act 70 of 2002. The full acronym should really read ROICAPOCRIA but it has become known as the 'RIC Act'.
213. *Supra* 31.
214. *Supra* 612ff.
215. Act 65 of 1996 and see *supra* 613ff.

Part IV. Intellectual Rights ('Digital Rights')

Chapter 1. Patent Law (Applied to Software, Hardware and Other Patentable Goods)

§1. Introduction

231. With regard to the law of patent, South Africa should be seen in the wider context of the entire continent of Africa, and particularly the ties that many countries still have with their former colonial masters. In Africa, a pronounced split exists between members of the British Commonwealth and the francophone countries. Even though an African Intellectual Property Organization (AIPO) has existed since 1962, located in Yaoundé in the United Republic of Cameroon, its activities are mostly limited to French-speaking countries in Africa. A rival organization entitled the African Regional Industrial Property Organization (ARIPO) has come into being, with its headquarters in Harare, Zimbabwe.

232. In an interesting article, Alan J.S. Dunlop discusses South Africa's options in the context of broader cooperation in the field of patents. He feels that South Africa's strong economy, with its high rate of patent and design registrations, might be just what is needed to make ARIPO fully viable.[216]

233. On the other hand, in *Cyberlaw@SA III* at 130ff., the author of the chapter on patent [217] distinguishes three main arguments against using patents to legally protect software. These are that the South African Patent Office lacks the necessary expertise to guarantee the quality of patents in software, that such patents[218] might have a negative effect on the country's economy, and third that the nature of software and e-commerce business methods make patent protection inappropriate.

234. As has been mentioned in the General Introduction, the system of intellectual property law in South Africa is firmly based on British law. This is the result of a series of specific statutes in this regard, mostly based on the example in the

216. In *The South African Institute of Intellectual Property Law Newsletter* 58 (4 of 1998).
217. Caroline Ncube.
218. Including patents in e-commerce.

'mother country'. A notable exception to this rule is constituted by competition law, which is grounded on the Roman-Dutch law, as will be shown when dealing with this particular aspect of the law.[219]

235. In the case of patents, the main source of law is the South African Patents Act.[220] This Act is closely modelled on the British Patents Act; thus, South African courts have had regard to British case law, for instance, in the case of *Tolima (Pty) Ltd v. Cugacius Motor Accessories (Pty) Ltd.*[221] Even though the South African Act does not contain a definition of a patent, the South African Green Paper on Electronic Commerce[222] defined a patent as 'a document, issued by a government office, which describes the invention and creates a legal situation in which the patented invention can only by exploited (altered, used or sold) by, or with the authorization of the patentee'.

236. As far as international relationships are concerned, South Africa is a signatory to the Paris Convention or the International Convention for the Protection of Industrial Property. This provides that patents belonging to a national from one of the signatory countries will be protected in all the others. South Africa has also become part of the Patent Cooperation Treaty, which provides for 'international applications' to be made at a 'receiving office', which could be in the applicant's own country. Such an application then gives the applicant a one-year option to decide whether he (or she) wants to make the claim permanent by also pursuing it in the other treaty countries. In order to comply with its treaty obligations South Africa has passed legislation in the form of Chapter V of the Intellectual Property Amendment Act.[223]

§2. The Position in South Africa and in a Comparative Context

237. How does the above legal situation apply specifically to the patenting of computer hardware and software in South Africa? As far as hardware is concerned, no formal bar exists. In practice, however, not very many original applications are developed in South Africa. This does not mean, of course, that countries with such developments would not have a great interest in protecting their patent rights in South Africa. During the apartheid era in South Africa, restrictions were placed by many countries on the export of sophisticated computer technology to South Africa, for fear that this technology might be used by the South African Defence Force and the police services.

---

219. See *infra.*
220. Act 57 of 1978. For more extensive commentary, *see also* Van der Merwe et al., *ICT Law* (2022), 39ff.
221. 1983 (3) SA 504 (E).
222. Privately published by the SA Department of Communications (November 2000) at 44, *see also* Buys (ed.), *Cyberlaw@SA* II (2004), 62. A Green Paper is usually a prelude to legislation, yet the only aspect of IP that was covered by the resulting ECT Act 25 of 2002, was the question of domain names.
223. Act 38 of 1997.

238. As far as software is concerned, the South African Patents Act[224] specifically excludes a computer program from being regarded as a patentable invention. Section 25(3) of this act, however, states that the prohibition relates only to the thing *as such*. In LAWSA,[225] it has been suggested that South Africa might be informed by the interpretation of the corresponding sections[226] in the European Patent Convention. South African academics have debated the precise meaning of the term 'as such' in this limitation. According to Coenraad Visser,[227] one should distinguish two situations clearly. If a patent is sought on a computer program operating on its own, this would be 'as such' and this is obviously prohibited by the Patents Act. On the other hand, if computer technology is utilized as part of a 'special device', the latter may still be granted a patent even though a computer program is thus granted indirect protection. The author gives two examples:

> where the computer program is encoded in the memory matrix of a semiconductor chip (in other words, the so-called firmware) or in the case of 'apparatus claims' where it is argued that the combination of a general purpose digital computer and the computer program results in a new special-purpose apparatus with the capacity to perform the object of the program.

239. In a later UK case, namely *Aerotel Ltd v. Telco Holdings Ltd*,[228] the court laid down the following four-stage test to determine whether a given invention should be patentable. These requirements are:

(1) proper construal of the claim;
(2) identification of the actual contribution;
(3) determination whether such actual contribution falls within any excluded subject matter; and
(4) determination whether the actual or alleged contribution is actually technical in nature.

240. Because the patent was for a computer program, it was excluded in terms of ground (3) above, even though the program drove an interactive website.

241. The South African Patents Act poses two requirements before registration may take place. These are 'novelty' and 'inventive step'. The latter requirement means that the new idea should not have been too obvious to a person skilled in the area in which the patent application is submitted.[229] This may present problems as far as information technology is concerned because most inventions 'stand on the shoulders of those that had gone before'. For this reason, it is probably a good thing that the requirement is only a further 'step' in the journey of invention. A good

224. Act 57 of 1978.
225. *Patents Inventions and Heraldry* 20 (1984), §6.
226. Sections 52 and 57.
227. C Visser in SALJ 100 (1983): 755, 756.
228. [2006] EWCA] Civ 1371.
229. Section 3 of Act 57 of 1978.

example of an inventive step as far as software is concerned would be the use of the 'Java' object-oriented programming language.[230]

242. The requirement of novelty presents its own problems. In the South African case of *Meter Patent Development (Pty) Ltd v. Ash Electronic Industries & Another*,[231] the latter party (formerly called Altec) had assigned a patent to the former party (formerly called Spescom) in a new invention. This was a 'credit supply system' that involved the encryption and matching of codes. The assignment had been granted by the Patent Office but Meter now applied for an amendment in the patent, specifically to address the problem of novelty. The problem had arisen because of the registration of wide-ranging patents overseas by Schlumberger and Sloan. The defendant, Ash, asked the court for a total revocation of the patent. This request was held over until the matter of the amendment had been dealt with. Taking all circumstances into account, Judge van Dijkhorst granted the amendment but it is not reported what happened to the matter of revocation.

243. Commentators have bemoaned the relative lack of importance of patent in the South African information technology sector. Wendy Rachmim[232] mentions two factors as possible causes for this state of events. In the first place, she argues that 'inventors have no clarity as to when a computer program is a computer program as such'[233] and that this uncertainty has a stifling effect on the patenting of programs. The second problem is one that besets more than one field in informatics law, namely the jurisdictional problems which may arise in such an international field. It is of no use having a patent that is perfectly valid and legal and registered, if no legal infrastructure exists to enforce that patent against 'repeat infringers' in China, some Pacific islands or other 'cyber-havens'.[234] The only real solution to this problem is to engage all other international role players in reciprocal treaties according to which 'I will catch (and extradite) your infringers if you will do the same with mine'.

§3. Patent and Standards with Regard to New Business Methods and Data Formats[235]

244. In contradistinction to South Africa and Europe, where patenting software is generally not allowed, the US has happily turned to patenting not only software but also firmware, business methods, and data formats such as XML[236] and

230. 'Java' was originally called 'oak' because the 'inventor' was inspired and consoled by the sight of an oak tree growing outside his office window!
231. Burrell's *Patent Law Reports* (1995): 185.
232. *See* W. Rachmim, in Buys (ed.), *Cyberlaw@SA* (2000), 75.
233. *See* the discussion of this requirement *supra*.
234. Here I am thinking of Monaco and similar countries which have earned a reputation as 'tax havens' or 'tax shelters' because of their specific taxation regimes.
235. *See* Van der Merwe et al., *ICT Law* (2022), 62ff.
236. *See* Van der Merwe et al., *ICT Law* (2022), 63ff.

XBRL.[237] Especially in the case of XML, this led to patent disputes on an international scale and increased pressure on South African patent authorities to allow such patents in South Africa.[238] This was particularly the case with regard to a Microsoft 'dialect' of XML, called OOXML,[239] the patenting of which the adherents of open standards XML were trying to block. One can now safely say that this battle has lost all business relevance, particularly in the light of the rise of XBRL as the standard of choice for the exchange of business information.

245. Most of the above matters have been explored in greater detail in an article by the present author entitled 'XBRL and the Law: Legal Implications of Markup Languages[240] as well as one by Peter Visagie entitled 'South African Patent Office's Recent Grant for and Invention Created by Artificial Intelligence'.[241] The latter article introduces one of the components of the so-called Fourth Industrial Revolution[242] Some of the other topics brought about by this 'revolution' include self-driving vehicles (such as TESLA), robotics as well as 'the Internet of Things'.

237. Xtensible Business Reporting Language.
238. *Ibid.*,.
239. Open Office XML.
240. 74 THRHR (2011) 418ff.
241. See 'AI as inventor' at http://mondaq.com.
242. *See* Van der Merwe et al., *ICT Law* (2022), 65.

Chapter 2. Trademarks (Application in the Digital Context)

§1. Trademark Protection: An Introduction

246. Although sounding similar and also being part of intellectual property rights, trademarks differ appreciably from trade secrets. They probably have more in common with patents, being statutory and giving the holder worldwide legal protection against any other claimant, in return for registering[243] with a central authority. The same could be said about the protection of designs; in fact, these probably have even more in common with patents, as well as often overlapping substantially with copyright protection. Nevertheless, judged on the deeper philosophical ground of promoting fair competition in trade, the law of trademarks and the law of designs carry out exactly the same function as the law of trade secrets.

247. One should bear in mind that the original treaty dealing with international patent also made provision for the protection of trademarks.[244] It is important to also understand that there has been a groundswell movement towards treating intellectual property rights as a trade-related issue and thus moving it into the world of General Agreement on Tariffs and Trade (GATT) and Trade-Related Aspects of Intellectual Property Rights (TRIPS). This has led to a corresponding lessening of importance of the traditional standard-setting bodies such as World Intellectual Property Organization (WIPO) and the older IP treaties – primarily the Berne Convention and the Universal Copyright Convention for copyright and the Paris Convention for patents and trademarks. As a result of (mainly US) pressure, a World Trade Organization (WTO) has come into being and by becoming a member a country also has to assume certain responsibilities, through TRIPS, with regard to IP, including trademark and design rights.

248. Trademarks existed from about 4,000 years ago and have traditionally served the following functions:

249. First, they served as a form of advertising, allowing makers to get their name in front of potential customers. Second, they may have been used to prove that the goods were sold by a particular merchant, thus helping to resolve ownership disputes. Third, the marks served as a guarantee of quality, since a merchant who identifies herself with her goods puts her reputation on the line.[245]

250. These functions and objectives remain valid well into the twenty-first century, when we have grown accustomed to the brave new world of electronic commerce.[246]

243. Although in many jurisdictions a trademark may be also be obtained by mere use.
244. The Paris Convention on Industrial Property of 1883. A number of succeeding 'Paris' Conventions have been held since, in various other cities.
245. Merges, Menell, Lemley & Jorde, *Intellectual Property in the New Technological Age* (Aspen, 1997) at 523.
246. This statement comprises both traditional e-commerce as well as the more recent 'm-commerce'.

251. According to B.R. Rutherford,[247] the 1963 South African Trade Marks Act had been badly in need of reform, having been in force for nearly thirty years. He also stresses the need to conform to international developments, particularly the European Directive on Trade Marks and the TRIPS requirements of the Uruguay Round of the GATT negotiations (both discussed in the previous section). UK has enacted a new Trade Mark Act in 1994 to bring that country in line with the European directive. As the UK is one of South Africa's major trading partners it was important for South Africa to also get in line. The TRIPS agreement is also South Africa's passport to international trade and many of the TRIPS requirements in fact overlap with those of the European directive.

252. The later Act[248] is then described by Rutherford as 'South Africa's attempt to modernize its trademark system and to keep abreast of the international developments mentioned above'. With this statement, he encompasses the European directive, the 1994 UK Act as well as the TRIPS requirements.

§2. WHAT IS A TRADEMARK?

253. The term 'trademark' is defined as:

> A mark used or proposed to be used by a person in relation to goods or services for the purpose of distinguishing the goods or services in relation to which the mark is used or proposed to be used from the same kind of goods or services connected in the course of trade with any other person.[249]

254. By focusing on the distinguishing function instead of the original origin function, the definition is more in line with the international requirements as set out above. According to *Cyberlaw@SA* II,[250] the distinguishing function also plays a very important role with regard to advertising, because it creates 'brand awareness' among potential customers.

255. The term 'mark' has been defined (in the same section) as: 'any sign capable of being represented graphically, including a device, name, signature, word, letter, numeral, shape, configuration, pattern, ornamentation, colour or container for goods or any combination of the aforementioned'.

247. In B.R. Rutherford in Coenraad Visser (ed.), *The New Law of Trade Marks and Designs* (1995), 1. *See also* van der Merwe et al., *ICT Law* (Durban, 2022), 249ff.
248. Act 194 of 1993, in operation since 1 May 1995.
249. Section 1 of the South African Trade Marks and Designs Act 194 of 1993.
250. Buys (ed.) *Cyberlaw@SA* (2004), 30.

256. Rutherford is of the opinion that the above definition is not exhaustive and creates the potential for the registration of sounds,[251] and even smells, as trademarks. If it is this wide, a domain name under the Internet might perhaps also be included (*see* discussion below).

257. Buys et al.[252] comment that the above definition requires that a mark should be capable of being represented graphically. This would imply a visual representation such as by means of a 'photograph, drawing, painting, engraving, etching or a computer created representation or in writing'. Even though one should applaud the fact that a 'computer created representation' has been included, one should perhaps go further and indicate whether this should be printed out, or whether the digitally stored format would suffice.

§3. The Protection Rendered by Trademark Registration

258. A brief look at the rest of the act shows that by restricting infringement rights to goods or services in respect of which the trademark is actually used, the act has made 'defensive' registrations impossible. Anti-dilution provisions have also been brought in, prohibiting the use of another mark, which would be likely to take unfair advantage of, or be detrimental to, the distinctive character or repute of the registered mark.[253] Papadopoulos et al.[254] distinguish between dilution by blurring and dilution by tarnishment. The former dilutes the uniqueness of the distinctive nature of the trademark, and this may be done by a third party, that is, not one of the commercial competitors of the trademark registrant. Tarnishment happens when the trademark is brought into disrepute by being used in a negative or offensive way, for instance, by associating the trademark with apartheid, slavery, etc.

259. An interesting example in South Africa is the case of *South African Breweries International T/A Sabmark International v. Laugh It Off Promotions*[255] where the typical 'Black Label' beer getup is featured on a T-shirt with the stylized words now reading 'Black Labour – white guilt' and other examples of alleged exploitation of South African Blacks by South African Whites.[256] The producers of the t-shirt argued that they were simply lampooning or satirizing and that this fell within their constitutional rights of freedom of expression. After this argument failed to impress the court, they were restrained from proceeding with this and similar t-shirts. The court held that the respondent's right to freedom of artistic activity exceeded the limits of freedom of speech and speech afforded by the Constitution.

251. The exhaust note of a Harley Davidson motorcycle is very distinctive and has not yet been equalled by Japanese clones. Perhaps trademark protection or patent has had something to do with this.
252. Buys (ed.), *Cyberlaw@SA II* (2004), at 31.
253. Section 34(1)(c).
254. Snail and Papadopoulos (ed.), *Cyberlaw@SA III* (2012), at 199.
255. [2003] 2 All SA 454 (C).
256. *See* in general Van der Merwe et al., *ICT Law* (2022), 249ff.

Another part of the *ratio decidendi* was that the ads could be said to border on hate speech, which would infringe the provisions of the Promotion of Equality and Prevention of Unfair Discrimination Act.[257]

260. The matter went on appeal[258] on the same issues but *Laugh It Off* was again unsuccessful. The court held that their reliance on the defence of parody was misconceived. The appellants' use of the respondent's trademark on t-shirts was detrimental to the reputation of the mark and this amounted to an abuse of the right to freedom of speech. The appeal was, therefore, dismissed. As a final resort (literally), appellant turned to the Constitutional Court in the case of *Laugh It Off Promotions CC v. SAB International (Finance) BV* [259] where Moseneke J. held that section 34(1)(c) of the Trade Mark Act should be understood 'through the prism of the Constitution' and specifically in the light of the guarantee to freedom of expression.[260] Because no direct economic effect was experienced by the owner of the trademark, the appeal was successful. A warning word is sounded as to the emphasis on economic factors swaying the law to such an extent by the authors of ICT law.[261]

257. Act 4 of 2000.
258. In *Laugh It Off Promotions CC v. SAB International (Finance) BV 2005 (2) SA 46 (SCA)*, [2004] 4 All SA 151 (SCA).
259. 2006 (1) SA 144 (CC).
260. Paragraph 43 of the decision.
261. Van der Merwe, D.P. et al., *ICT Law* (2022), 266..

Chapter 3. Design Protection (Application to Digital Products)

261. The origin of design registration has been described by Aplin in the 7th edition of the work *Intellectual Property: Patents, Copyright, Trade Marks and Allied Rights:*[262]

> The origins of design registration stretch back to the earliest period of industrialization in some parts of the textile industry. The real impetus towards the modern system came in the 1830s. The poor quality of British industrial design, particularly when compared with the achievements of the French, incited middle-class radicals to press for a system of training designers and manufacturers to demand a more substantial legal monopoly.

262. This led to a Copyright of Designs Act in 1842, but even though the name might indicate that this was merely another category of copyright 'the need actually to prove that an alleged infringement was copied' was gradually done away with. According to Cornish,[263] the protection of designs acquired characteristics of the patent system and in 1875, the Patent Office took over the registration and administration of designs. This uneasy coexistence of copyright and a design right has immigrated to South Africa and has here assumed a life of its own.

263. An interesting footnote on design from an international perspective – even though the US has adopted a specific act towards protecting semiconductor chip design, most other countries try to protect this as part of their general design protection (which has remained rather underdeveloped in the United States).

264. South Africa received an updated Designs Act[264] in tandem with the Trademarks Act discussed above. According to M. le Roux in *The New Law of Trade Marks and Designs*,[265] this act was unique by clearly distinguishing between aesthetic and functional design. 'Aesthetic design' is defined as:

> any design applied to any article, whether for the pattern or the shape or the configuration or the ornamentation thereof, or for any two or more of these purposes, and by whatever means it is applied, having the features which appeal to and are judged solely by the eye, irrespective of the aesthetic quality thereof.[266]

262. Seventh ed. (2010) 599ff.
263. *Ibid.*, 487.
264. Act 195 of 1993, in force since 1 May 1995.
265. See W.R. Cornish (Aplin 7th edition) in the work *Intellectual Property: Patents, Copyright, Trade Marks and Allied Rights* 487.
266. Section 1(1)(i).

265. On the other hand, the term 'functional design' is defined as:

> any design applied to any article, whether for the pattern of the shape or the configuration thereof, or for any two or more of these purposes, and by whatever means it is applied, having features which are necessitated by the function which the article to which the design is applied is to perform, and includes an integrated circuit topography, a mask work and a series of mask works.

266. Whereas the prior act[267] had required for a functional design features 'dictated solely by the function', the later act requires features 'necessitated by the function which the article to which the design is applied is to perform'.[268] Whether this is such a major change is debatable, and this point has in fact been so debated in *The New Law of Trade Marks and Designs*.[269]

267. In the same work, the South African copyright expert, O.H. Dean, relates the sorry history of the 'interplay' (some would say, confusion) between copyright and design protection. This follows the unhappy history in the UK to a great extent (South Africa usually taking its lead from the UK in the field of IP) except for an interesting amendment in 1988. The full history is succinctly set out by Dean (also in *The New Law of Trade Marks and Designs*), and the following is a brief synopsis and attempt to link it with UK developments.

268. Besides the protection enjoyed in terms of the Designs Act, designs are also protected by section 1(1) of the Copyright Act[270] under the category of 'artistic work', which is defined[271] as meaning:

> irrespective of the artistic quality thereof:
>
> (a) paintings, sculptures, drawings, engravings and photographs;
> (b) works of architecture being either buildings or models of buildings;
> (c) works of craftsmanship not falling within either paragraph (a) or (b).

269. Things are not as they may seem on the surface, however. 'Drawings' are further defined as including 'any drawing of a technical nature or any diagram, map chart or plan'. According to Dean, an 'artistic work' includes visual representations of ideas or the results of intellectual effort in a material form. The 'drawings' and 'works of craftsmanship' categories would include design drawings of articles of manufacture or industrial products, and prototypes of such goods. 'Reproduction' with regard to an 'artistic work' (which is the category containing all these concepts) is defined to include making a three-dimensional from a two-dimensional version and vice versa. Making a reproduction of something that is already a

267. Act 57 of 1967.
268. Section 1(1)(xi).
269. In Coenraad Visser (ed.) *The New Law of Trade Marks and Designs* (1995), at 76–77.
270. Act 98 of 1978.
271. In s. 1(1) of the act.

manufactured reproduction of the original design or prototype (say an exhaust system for a motorcar) would constitute an indirect reproduction of the original copyrighted design or prototype.

270. The draughtsman of the 1916 Patents, Designs, Trade Marks and Copyrights Act[272] appreciated that a design might enjoy double protection and, therefore, provided that only if a design was not capable of registration as such, would it enjoy copyright protection. The question as to which designs were capable of registration or not, was discussed in the case of *Klep Valves (Pty) Ltd v. Saunders Valve Co Ltd.*[273]

271. By the time the 1965 Copyright Act came along, the idea was still to avoid double protection, but it was now done procedurally, rather than substantially. Dean explains this as follows:

> The 1965 Act did not provide that no copyright subsisted in artistic works that were capable of registration as designs. Rather, it limited the right of the owner of the copyright in a relevant artistic work to sue for infringement of copyright in certain circumstances. The copyright continued to exist but became partly unenforceable. Section 11 provided that such part of the copyright as would have fallen within the scope of a corresponding registered design became unenforceable and was in fact 'forfeited'. Case law established that the forfeiture of the enforceability of the copyright in an artistic work occurred only where the design of the article depicted in the work was capable of registration as a design; where the design of the article was dictated solely by the function which the article had to perform and so could not be registered as a design, the forfeiture did not take place.[274]

272. In other words, if the design was fit for registration in terms of the present Designs Act,[275] that part of copyright protection that was now no longer necessary (because of the design right protection) became unenforceable. The latest Copyright Act[276] did not initially carry over the unenforceability provisions of its predecessor but was amended in 1983 to again make copyright enforceable in certain circumstances. These were the following:

> when authorized three-dimensional reproductions of an artistic work had been made available to the public, inside or outside South Africa, and someone without the consent of the copyright owner made three-dimensional reproductions

272. Act 9 of 1916.
273. 1985 (1) SA 646 (T).
274. O.H. Dean in *The New Law of Trade Marks and Designs*, ed. Coenraad Visser (1995) at 80.
275. Act 57 of 1967.
276. Act 98 of 1978 (with its multiple amendments).

> or adaptations of that artistic work by copying the authorized three-dimensional reproductions or adaptations of that work, provided that the authorized reproductions which serve as the basis for the copying primarily have a utilitarian purpose and are made by an industrial process.[277]

273. This meant that a design could be reverse-engineered from the finished product (say a car's exhaust system) without the holder of the copyright in the design being able to enforce its rights. Initially this block on enforcement only came into effect within ten years of the passing of the act (1993) or ten years after the finished product had been placed on the market anywhere in the world, whichever date was the later. Thus, indirectly an overlap between the Copyright and Design Acts was avoided, although the Design Act was never mentioned by name. The ten-year delay for the block on enforcement was removed by a 1988 amendment of the Copyright Act,[278] and the latter would come into effect immediately after the finished product has been placed on the market anywhere in the world.[279]

274. The requirement of 'making by an industrial process' is fortunate because so many computer graphics and animations (and even full-length animated features and computer games) are rendered in a three-dimensional, yet virtual and pictorial, format these days. It was probably not the intention to treat these in the same fashion as manufactured articles by the common use of the word 'three-dimensional'. The latter term has now been overtaken by progress and should not be used in future legislation.

275. In summing up, Dean feels that copyright and design protection no longer complement each other and that each 'by itself leaves considerable scope for abuse of the manufacturer's position by competitors'. He feels that we should have followed the British and European Directives' lead in this regard.

276. In closing, a few words should be said about the protection of integrated circuits (ICs) or 'chips'. Since these fall into the category of a 'functional design', the new Designs Act should protect these circuits adequately, even though the Americans felt that they had to promulgate a specific act in this regard. C.K. Job, in the same work by Coenraad Visser cited above,[280] explains that even though the possibility existed of a sui generis right to protect ICs, or amendment of the Copyright Act in this regard, it was decided that the new Design Act would be the best vehicle in this regard:

277. Section 15(3A) of the Act.
278. Act 13 of 1988.
279. Perhaps a throwback to the South African sanctions era, when because of the international boycott, many things had to be locally produced.
280. C.K. Job in *The New Law of Trade Marks and Designs*, ed. Coenraad Visser (1995) at 90.

> After all, despite being somewhat specialized, complex and minute, integrated circuits and their topographies are merely designs having pattern, shape and configuration, and their features are necessitated by the functions which the integrated are to perform.

277. Thus, ICs and their corollaries, 'mask works' are now protected in South Africa as designs, complying in this fashion with this country's TRIPS obligations in this regard. In fact, we seem to have overshot, since TRIPS determines that a person will act lawfully if he did not know, or did not have reasonable ground to know, that the article concerned incorporated unlawfully produced layout designs. The equivalent South African liability is strict, in other words, not dependent on 'guilty knowledge'.

Chapter 4. Copyright Protection in the Digital Context (Including Software

§1. General Introduction

278. As has been pointed out above in General Introduction (Chapter 1, General Background of the Country), the South African fields of patent and copyright have, in the past, been modelled on those of the UK. This state of affairs has been confirmed by the South African judiciary in the case of *Tolima (Pty) Ltd v. Cugacius Motor Accessories (Pty) Ltd.*[281] The 'four cornerstones' of English copyright have been set out in their Statute of Anne[282] as follows:

(1) natural law;
(2) a return on labour and skill expended;
(3) an incentive to create; and
(4) the advancement of society.

279. The above-mentioned four principles are 'cumulative and interdependent and underpin the justification of copyright law in all countries'.[283] However, the true origin of copyright precedes the British developments of the eighteenth century by several centuries and coincides with the invention of the printing press in the fifteenth century by Johannes Gutenberg.[284]

280. South Africa has had an unfortunate history as a copyright pirate. This unhappy state of affairs stems from the days of the apartheid government when South Africa was the subject of an economic boycott by most of the rest of the world. The boycott included software products, so that if one could obtain a copy of the latest overseas software, this was seen as 'patriotism' or another way of 'beating the rest of the world'. Even though South Africa has been 'legalized' in many other respects since 1994, software piracy remains a huge problem. Organizations such as the Federation Against Software Theft (FAST) have been created in order to deal with the problem and do so by any means, from television adverts to auditing companies and organizations for the legality of their software. FAST operates by means of cooperation between the police as well as suppliers and distributors of software.

281. The South African law of copyright is basically contained in the much-amended, but still rather ancient, South African Copyright Act[285] with some (much-needed) amendments coming from the omnibus ECT Act,[286] especially as far as

281. 1983 (3) SA 504 (E).
282. The Copyright Act 1709 8 Anne, C.19 and *see* in general on copyright and digital content Van der Merwe et al., *ICT Law* (2022), 297ff.
283. *Ibid.*
284. See DP van der Merwe 'Copyright and Computers, with special reference to the Internet – From Penmanship to Peepshow' 115 SALJ 180 (1998).
285. Act 98 of 1978.
286. Act 25 of 2002.

domain names are concerned. In South Africa, registration is not a prerequisite to have legal copyright in something that one has created, except in the case of cinematographic films that include the digital formats, such as digital video disk (DVD). The Copyright Act prohibits certain actions, which are reserved to the copyright holder, unless these are exempted by its so-called fair dealing provisions. The so-called fair dealing provisions[287] allow certain actions, which would otherwise have constituted copyright infringements. Fair dealing occurs when a reproduction is made for purposes of research or private study, for criticism of the work or for the purposes of reporting current events.

282. In the case of computer programs, the 'research and study' exemption falls away,[288] but copies are allowed for personal and private backup purposes, provided they are destroyed when ownership of the main program becomes unlawful.

283. As may be noted from the above, not all copyright products are the same. The South African Copyright Act[289] splits the different types of protected work into watertight compartments. These consist of a 'literary work',[290] an 'artistic work', a 'musical work', a 'computer program', a 'sound recording', a 'cinematographic film', a 'sound and television broadcast', a 'program-carrying signal', and a 'published edition'. One of the shortcomings of this rigid categorization has been the uncertain position of a later category such as 'multimedia works'. In the present time of convergence of media, especially on the Internet, a rigid and limited classification of this nature may lead to many legal uncertainties. The same might be said for the new copyright category of databases, the latter forming the backbone of the present 'Information Age'. South Africa has followed the route of expediency by including databases under the category of 'literary works', classifying them under the sub-category of 'tables and compilations'.[291]

284. Even more[292] than with patent, one needs an international dimension and an eye on international regulation when dealing with the law pertaining to copyright. In this regard, the Berne Convention for the Protection of Literary and Artistic Works[293] plays an important role. It is administered by the World Intellectual Property Organization (WIPO), a United Nations agency based in Geneva, Switzerland, which specializes in this subject area. South Africa acceded to the Berne Convention in 1928, and traditionally, copyright holders could look to this Convention for the protection of their intellectual property rights. Can they still avail themselves of this right in the world of digital 'property'?

287. Contained in s. 12 of Act 98 of 1978. *See also infra* for a more in-depth discussion of 'fair use'.
288. Section 19B of Act 98 of 1978.
289. Section 2(1).
290. Even though a pre-statute court decision put a computer program firmly into the category of a 'literary work' – *see Northern Office Microcomputers (Pty) Ltd v. Rosenstein*1981 (4) SA 123 (C).
291. *See* the definition of 'literary work' in s. 1 of the Act, para. (g). Note too that 'computer programs' are specifically excluded from the definition of a literary work.
292. Because patent has a registration requirement, its international dimensions are easier to manage.
293. Downloadable at <www.law.cornell.edu/treaties/berne/overview.html>.

285. One of the major problems with the Berne Convention is its absence of effective enforcement mechanisms, a common problem with some international instruments that have been built on an assumption of international cooperation and goodwill among nations. In this regard, the Trade Related Aspects of Intellectual Property Rights (TRIPS) Agreement, which binds all members of the World Trade Organization (WTO), may be of interest. In April 1994, South Africa became a member of the WTO and acceded to the TRIPS Agreement. Because so many of the subject areas which TRIPS are supposed to govern are now in digital format and/or appear on the Internet, the Member States of WIPO passed two so-called Internet treaties on 20 December 1996, namely the WIPO Copyright Treaty (WCT) and the WIPO Performances and Phonogram Treaty.[294] It is an open question whether the South African Copyright Act, in its present format, complies with the stringent treaty requirements that are now applicable to this country.

§2. The Subsistence of Copyright

286. The basic question to be determined with regard to copyright is whether copyright exists with regard to a given article. This is also known as the question of subsistence. It is, of course, more problematical than is the case with patents, because only the latter have a prescribed registration system that facilitates proof, priority, etc. When one deals with the copyright in digital objects, the situation is much worse because of the ease with which such objects or even just small parts thereof, may be copied and disseminated by means of the Internet.

287. It is mostly accepted in South Africa that one does not have copyright in a mere idea, but that one should embody that idea in some form of creative utterance such as a book, a musical work or the like.

288. In this regard, an interesting argument has been made by A.J.C. Copeling, who argues that copyright does exist in ideas:

> Yet, 'skill' and 'judgment' are qualities of the mind and devoid of any physical attribute. Indeed, in the context in which they are referred to by the courts, they are simply complementary parts of the literary concept or idea which gives rise to and later becomes embodied in the eventual compilation.[295]

289. From the above quotation, it seems clear that the author does require an embodiment of the author's skill and judgment in some 'compilation', which is obviously more concrete than a mere idea. Nonetheless, Copeling does well to draw attention to the fact that it is not just the coincidental format of the work itself that deserves copyright protection, but that the mental labour and creativity of a human brain are really the qualities that should be rewarded by the law.

---

294. *See* Buys (ed.), *Cyberlaw@SA* (2004), 2.
295. 'Copyright in Ideas' 28 THRHR (1965): 3 ff.

290. According to the South African Copyright Act,[296] the 'ownership'[297] of any work vests in the author. A statutory exception is, however, built into the Copyright Act itself.[298]

291. Where in a case not falling within either (b) or (c)[299] a work is made in the course of the author's employment by another person under a contract or service or apprenticeship, that other person shall be the owner of any copyright subsisting in the work by virtue of section 3 or 4.

292. Who is the 'author' of a computer program? According to the South African Copyright Act,[300] it is the person who exercises control over the making of the computer program. This obviously covers the multi-skilled team that is needed for major software project nowadays but would probably also cover the poor 'hacker' sitting alone at his or her keyboard during the midnight hours, creating a program single-handedly. According to a South African decision, *Haupt T/A Softcopy v. Brewers Marketing Intelligence (Pty) Ltd and Others*,[301] the concept of 'control' as far as determining the authors of computer programs are concerned is wider than the 'control' exercised by an employer over employees in terms of section 21(1)(d) of the South African Copyright Act.[302]

293. With regard to 'a literary, dramatic, musical or artistic work or computer program which is computer-generated' on the other hand, the author is 'the person by whom the *arrangements* necessary for the creation of the work were undertaken'.[303] The only apparent difference with regard to a computer program (*see* the previous paragraph) and, therefore, also the difference between 'control' and 'arrangements', respectively, seems to be that for purposes of the present paragraph, the author seems to have washed his or her hands of the whole creative process itself, leaving 'control' to the computer (and perhaps the program) 'to do its own thing'.

§3. The Scope of Copyright

I. General

294. According to one commentator, the legal problems that fall under this heading are even more intractable than those dealing with the subsistence of copyright:

---

296. Act 98 of 1978, s. 21(1)(a).
297. The term 'ownership' is used in a qualified sense. In South African legal theory one may only own something to which a real right exists, usually a tangible object. The copyright 'owner' really only has an immaterial property right to patents, copyrighted items, trademarks, etc.
298. Section 21(1)(d).
299. Both subsections dealing with non-computer-related works.
300. Act 98 of 1978, the definition of 'author' in s. 1, para. (i).
301. 2006 (4) SA 458 (SCA).
302. Act 98 of 1978.
303. Section 1, para. (h) of the definition of 'author'.

the problems experienced in determining the scope of copyright protection in the present context, would make those experienced in relation to the subsistence of copyright in software, look pale in comparison.[304]

295. Basically, what is understood under 'scope' by the present author is exactly how wide does one's right go, once one has established one's right?

II. Adaptation and Translation

296. In some of the first proposals made to bring the South African Copyright Act[305] in line with the world of IT, Piet Burger[306] suggested that the term 'adaptation' should include 'translation' and that both these activities should be reserved for the copyright holder. He also suggested that a third program, created by the interaction between two other programs, should also be included within the scope of the term 'adaptation'.

297. Section 1 of the present South African Copyright Act now defines 'adaptation' of a computer program to include:

(i) a version of the program in a programming language, code or notation different from that of the program;[307]
(ii) a fixation of the program in or on a medium different from the medium of fixation of the program.

298. Although the present text would seem to take care of Burger's translation argument, it does not give clarity to the question of a new program created by interaction between existing programs. Even though section 11B(c) of the present Copyright Act expressly vests in the copyright holder the exclusive right to reproduce or publish an 'adaptation' of the program, what happens to independent purchasers of a program who then use that program to create something new, which might be a composite of different cooperating programs? This aspect will be discussed under the following heading.

---

304. (1984) CILSA 32.
305. Act 98 of 1978.
306. A copyright attorney, addressing the Computer Society of South Africa (CSSA) on 1 Oct. 1985 in Johannesburg.
307. Extended definition explained in *Apple Computer Inc v. Rosy T/A Computer Comptronic Corporation and Another 134 JOC (D)* and *Sophisticated Design (Pty) Ltd v. Jensen Electronics (Pty) Ltd* (unreported TPD case no. 13088/89).

III. Use (or Transient Reproduction)

299. Because computer random access memory (CRAM)[308] is usually volatile, this used to mean that whenever a computer is off, the working copy of say, a word-processing document, simply vanishes. That is the reason why users are always warned to save copies of their working documents as work progresses. Upon the start of a fresh working session, a saved copy of the document had to be reloaded into the computer memory before work on it could start again.[309] The importance of this slightly technical explanation is that a copy or reproduction of a document is made every time that it is used on a computer. The question to the field of copyright is, therefore, whether the above-mentioned 'use'-copy should fall within the copyright restrictions on making copies of documents. To put it simply, in order to use anything on a computer, one has to accept that the computer will make a copy of it into its random access memory (RAM).[310] Would (and should) this 'copy' have any relevance for the Copyright Act?

300. This problem referred to in the previous paragraph was already raised but not resolved, at the 1996 Geneva Conference which led to the WCT. A draft article was put forward which was supposed to deal with rights of reproduction; however, this was withdrawn after strong reservations were expressed by some delegates, especially those representing librarians. This article would have reserved rights to the copyright owner that included the right to authorize 'direct and indirect reproduction . . . whether permanent or temporary, in any manner or form'. This solution might have solved the controversy once and for all, namely that the copyright holder would have to authorize even the temporary reproductions which are required to store or view a work in a digital format. However, a provision of this nature would also slow down the access to information on the Internet considerably. The following limitation on the need to obtain permission was then proposed by the sponsors:

> In cases where a temporary reproduction has the sole purpose of making the work perceptible or where the reproduction is of a transient or incidental nature, provided that such a reproduction takes place in the course of the work that is authorized by the author or permitted by law.

301. The final amendment mentioned in the previous paragraph was still not acceptable to the librarian lobby and the proposed article was omitted from the final treaty. The exception was thought to be too narrow and likely to be open to differing interpretations internationally.

---

308. 'RAM' from now on.
309. Using the very latest technology this is no longer necessary. The author's present Apple MacBook no longer has a magnetic hard drive because data may be saved onto a built-in memory chip forming part of the hardware and may be backed up either onto removable media such as a memory stick, or onto the 'cloud'.
310. Another problem under the present heading of 'use', is that of the cooperation between program, or between a program and a database, for instance.

302. In the view of the author of an article entitled 'Choice of law in Internet copyright dispute',[311] the proposed Geneva article might not even have been necessary. In his view, persons permitting their work to be available on the Internet are tacitly agreeing to the making of the transient copy necessary for viewing, although not necessarily for the making of copies onto another medium. This would be roughly equivalent to the abortive Article 7 discussed in the previous paragraphs, but would also be in conflict with one of Lee & Davidson's[312] 'laws of copyright' on the Internet:

> Do not assume that any material posted is public domain, particularly since the 1989 amendment to the Copyright Act makes it clear that lack of a copyright notice does not affect whether copyright subsists in a work.

303. Based on the above observations, a wise recommendation would seem to be that people should include 'terms of use' agreements with anything that they publish on the Internet or any other domain to which the public has a right of access. In this regard, the licences provided by the creative commons initiative[313] might be valuable. This initiative presents an interesting counterpart to the traditional world of copyright law where the flow of information is restricted as much as possible, unless the required payment is provided. Creative commons might encourage the free flow and transfer of information, which outcome is surely what the original concept of the Internet (and even of information technology in general) was all about.

304. The counterpart to the recommendation made at the beginning of the previous paragraph is, of course, that one should be careful to read any 'rights of use' notices appearing on websites. Failing to do so, might lead to (expensive) legal consequences that the user of that website had never considered.

§4. Duration and Infringement of Copyright

305. Normally, South African copyright survives the death of the author by fifty years.[314] In the case of computer programs (together with cinematographic films and photographs), the fifty years start running from the end of the year in which the work is made available to the public with the consent of the author, or failing such an event, within fifty years from the end of the year in which the work was made.[315] This is of course a very long period for a computer program to retain its usefulness or even to be available at the end of the period, and seems only to indicate a lack of familiarity with computer programs on the part of the legislature.

311. Coenraad Visser, *SA Mercantile Law Journal* 11 (1999), 286ff.
312. L.C. Lee & J.S. Davidson, *Intellectual Property for the Internet* (Wiley Law Publications, 1999).
313. *See* <www.creativecommons.org> in this regard.
314. Copyright Act 98 of 1977 s. 3(2)(a) and *see* Van der Merwe et al., *ICT Law* (2022), 40.
315. Section 3(2)(b).

306. Infringement might take place in the form of either direct or indirect (or secondary) infringement. The first form of infringement is committed by: 'a person, not being the owner of the copyright, who, without the license of such owner, does or causes any other person to do, in the Republic, any act which the owner has the exclusive rights to authorise'.[316]

307. Secondary infringement, on the other hand, includes such actions as: 'importing an (infringing) article into the Republic for any purpose other than his private and domestic use';[317] selling, letting, or exposing for trade such article;[318] distributing such article in the Republic to the prejudice of the owner;[319] or if he or she 'acquires an article relating to a computer program in the Republic',[320] with guilty knowledge regarding the infringement of copyright in respect of that particular article.

308. The final act prohibited in the previous paragraph leaves one with a bit of a legal conundrum. Does the prohibition on acquiring mean that the (guilty) possessors of an illicit copy of a computer program would fall within the words of the prohibition? If this is so, one wonders at the many second-hand stores[321] in South Africa having shelves filled with 'slightly used' second-hand software, available for sale. This kind of transaction obviously falls far outside of the original licensing terms by means of which the first buyer obtained the software.

309. For the very worst category of cases, the South African Copyright Act determines that even criminal sanctions may be imposed for copyright infringements.[322] These sanctions are quite stringent, with a first offence garnering a fine not exceeding (South African rand) ZAR 5,000 or imprisonment not exceeding three years, or both such fine and imprisonment *for each article* to which the offence relates. For second or further offenders, the maxima are pushed up to ZAR 10,000 or five years' imprisonment, or both, again for each article to which the offence relates.[323] Because most copyright victims would like to receive some personal recompense, large parts of the act are geared towards facilitating civil action in order to recover damages from the copyright offenders.

§5. The Rapid Development of Technology: Implications for Copyright

310. In the Middle Ages, copying a book was a process undertaken by monks, a task which usually consumed about half a lifetime of the poor copier. There was no need for a division of law called copyright, because no doubt existed as to who

316. Section 23(1) of Act 98 of 1978.
317. Section 23(2)(a).
318. Section 23(2)(b).
319. Section 23(2)(c).
320. Section 23(2)(d).
321. Such as 'Cash Converters' (a South African second-hand goods store).
322. Section 27.
323. Section 27(6) of the Act.

exactly possessed the rights to the laboriously crafted copy. This situation changed rapidly with the invention of movable typesetting and the printing press by Gutenberg and Caxton. Suddenly hundreds of copies could be run off on a day, which brought down the cost of a copy of a book or manuscript by many factors. Not only the monks were threatened by these new inventions, but also the original authors who found that other people were now profiting from the authors' creative labour.

311. A similar position obtained when the photocopying machine (so beloved of modern students) was invented. Even though libraries had to post prominent copyright notices on their machines[324] and a number of authors probably lost some royalties, this machine did not threaten the very fabric of the copyright edifice. The same may be said for microfilm and microfiche technology.

312. The earth-shaking event for copyright occurred with the coming of computers and especially with the coming of a digital storage format. The impact of digital technology has been explained as follows:

> What does 'digital' mean, exactly? It means that books, paintings, music, film, databases, documents and many other kinds of intellectual property may be reduced to binary digits which represent a series of 'on and off switches' comprehensible to a computer only. By means of the computer, the original work may then be stored, modified, reproduced or even broadcast on, for instance the Internet. It makes nonsense of the different categories of intellectual property still adhered to in copyright legislation, since in digital form the different works may be integrated with each other to form a so-called 'multimedia' product, which combines text, pictures, sound and video.[325]

313. The very idea of separate categories of copyrighted material, based on the different underlying technologies, has, therefore, become outmoded. Nevertheless, the South African Copyright Act, as is the case with similar legislation overseas, still sticks to these different categories as if they constituted Holy Writ. Even the title for this area of law is fast becoming irrelevant, since even switching on a computer and taking a tour of the Internet involves the making of thousands of ephemeral 'copies'. Computers and other digital equipment usually function by making a working copy in their RAM memory, modifying that and then saving the amended result to a more permanent form of storage such as a memory stick, a magnetic hard drive on a computer, a magnetic tape, a Disk, Read-Only Memory (CD-ROM), an optical disk, or a DVD. The latter three are all examples of digital media. The difference in quality is easily seen when contrasting the (jumpy) low-focus image delivered by ordinary brown videotape and the crystal-clear clarity of DVD disks, which are stable, bright, well-defined and may be 'frozen' for indefinite periods of time.

324. In order to escape liability for unauthorized copying.
325. See van der Merwe, *Computers and the Law* (Juta, 2000), 44–45.

314. A recent digital phenomenon has been dubbed 'The Fourth Industrial Revolution' (4IR). In contrast to Alvin Toffler's work *The Third Wave* (consisting of land, industry and IT) the 4IR consists of four stages consisting of Stage 1 (general mechanization and the introduction of steam power), Stage 2 (mass production using electrical power) and Stage 3 (bringing about automated production, computers and robotics). Stage 4 is the very latest and is bringing about smart factories, autonomous production, machine learning and the 'Internet of Things (IoT).[326]

315. Is South African copyright law in any shape to deal with the coming of digital technology? Continental readers should take note of the fact that South Africa falls more into the Anglo-American tradition of intellectual property, which sees copyright simply as an economic right to something that may be bought and sold irrevocably. This is widely known as the 'common-law tradition'[327] as opposed to the 'civil-law tradition' described in the next paragraph.

316. The European mainland view of copyright is that of a natural right of authors as part of their personality, which right can never be alienated either physically or legally. This point of view is more idealistic and believes that copyright should encourage creativity and the development of knowledge. It is known as the 'civil-law' concept of copyright.[328]

317. Nonetheless, these two historically disparate traditions will simply have to learn to work together in the new digital world of the Internet, which knows neither national nor continental boundaries. International cooperation by means of universally accepted and supported treaties are probably the only way to protect whatever is left of the right of the original author of an Internet publication. For this reason, it is of the utmost importance for Africa to 'get its act together' in order to protect its own heritage and to start making use (lawfully) of other sources of intellectual property. Perhaps this continent might even have an advantage when it comes to repealing outmoded laws and legislating more modern rules of intellectual property. After all, as a newcomer to the brave new digital world, it is not carrying so much historical baggage as most other countries do in this regard.

§6. Different Categories of Copyrightable Works

318. The South African Copyright Act differentiates between different categories of protected work, as does its 'mother' system in the UK. As has been mentioned before, the borders between these fields have become less well-defined because all these works are nowadays available in digital format.

326. *See also* Van der Merwe et al., *ICT Law* (2022), 119–120 and especially 384-385 for a fuller explanation of these new concepts.
327. *See* Helge M. Sonneland, '*Introduction to Copyright*', Paper read at the IFLA (International Federation of Librarians and Archivists) Pre-conference seminar, held at Tianjin, China during August 1996.
328. *Ibid.*

319. South African courts (not all of them computer literate), have struggled with the overlap between categories of digital copyright works. In the case of *Rapid Phase Enterprises v. SABC*,[329] the court was confronted with cartoon strip popular in South Africa entitled 'Madam and Eve'. After long deliberation, the court decided to place this work into the category of a 'work of art' even though the strip definitely tells a story. In the case of *Golden China TV Game Centre v. Nintendo*,[330] the court had to decide which category would best suit a video game. In the end, it decided against the (relatively) new category of 'computer program' and decided that it was a 'cinematographic film', thus negating the role of the processor in the game console entirely.

320. The case of *Pastel Software v. Pink Software (Pty) Ltd* [331] presents a particularly sorry example of digital copyright law. The matter turned on a new accounting package that was being marketed by a start-up company, Pink Software. An older software company, Pastel Software, claimed that the new package infringed its copyright in an existing, and well-known, accounting package. Pink had made quite sure that it had not copied any part of the program itself, which had been programmed by its own programmers. However, in order to make it easier to use for ex-Pastel users to use, Pink had used a similar-looking screen interface to the Pastel product. The judge had heard of the 'look and feel' test of US copyright courts, but unfortunately applied this test rather creatively. The real 'look and feel' test meant that if the structure and nature of the coding in one computer program was basically the same as the coding in another computer program, even though some minor changes may have been made, then the first program infringed copyright in the second program. The judge in the local case simply compared the two screens rendered by the different programs and declared that the one screen had the 'look and feel' of the other, and that, therefore, Pink had infringed Pastel's copyright in the computer program itself. This seems unsound, since the screen designs fall into quite another copyright category entirely (probably 'works of art') to which the 'look and feel' programming test would not apply.

321. It would appear that the whole copyright system (not only in South Africa) is in need of a rethink in the light of its struggle to adapt to the digital medium. More and more software companies are building technical protection into the medium itself, rather than relying on the rather spotty protection provided by the law. Here one thinks of digital watermarks on the medium itself or disks that can only be copied a limited number of times before they copy-protect themselves.

329. 597 JOC (W).
330. 1997 (1) SA 405 (E).
331. 399 JOC (1993) (T). *See also* Van der Merwe et al., *ICT Law* (2022), 321 and 334..

§7. Copyright and Its Application Regarding the Internet

I. The Internet

322. One of the first and most basic problems arises from the technical and legal question as to whether one makes a copy when one downloads a file from the Internet.[332] This prickly pear was raised but not resolved, at a Geneva conference convened to deal with this issue among others. This was a meeting of Council of the European Communities and the outcome was a Directive on the Legal Protection of Computer Programs.[333] The directive determined, *inter alia*, that computer programs should be protected in the same category as literary works, that only the expression is protected and not the idea behind it, and that the program has to be original. Other articles deal with authorship and the beneficiaries of copyright protection and define the rights that are exclusive to the copyright holder and that need to be authorized by the latter.

323. Article 5 of the directive removes certain activities from the purview of authorization by the holder, Article 6 deals with decompilation and the original Article 7 was to have dealt with a 'Right to Reproduction'.[334] This would have reserved the right to the copyright holder to authorize even the temporary reproductions, which are required to store work in a digital format in an electronic medium. This was opposed by a strong lobby of delegates, fronted by the librarians, because the delay involved in authorizing each such transient reproduction would have slowed down traffic on the Internet considerably. It was argued that the exception allowed to the proposed rule were too narrow and likely to be open to differing interpretations internationally. In the end, the librarians won the day and the proposed article was not adopted.

324. How has this turn of events affected South Africa? According to a local expert on copyright, persons permitting their copyright works to be placed onto the Internet are tacitly agreeing to the transient reproduction thereof necessary for viewing.[335] This would seem to support the abortive proposal discussed in the previous paragraph, but runs against one of Lee & Davidson's[336] 'laws of copyright in the Internet': 'Do not assume that any material posted is public domain, particularly since the 1989 amendment to the Copyright Act makes clear that lack of a copyright notice does not affect whether copyright subsists in a work'.

325. A second major question with regard to web copyright is who, exactly, 'owns' that copyright. Here the relevant clauses with regard to 'authorship', 'control', and 'arrangements' discussed under paragraphs 114 et seq. would come into

332. *See* in general Van der Merwe et al., *ICT Law* (2022), 318ff.
333. The meeting was held on 14 May 1991 and the directive was 91/250/EEC.
334. The present article merely deals with rights of rental after the original proposers were forced to withdraw their proposal to deal with a right to reproduction.
335. Although not for saving to disk, or making printouts. The expert is Coenraad Visser, *SA Mercantile Law Journal* 11 (1999): 268ff.
336. In *Intellectual Property for the Internet* (Wiley Law Publications, 1997), 141.

play. Unfortunately, these provisions do not always dispose of the question. The problem is basically that a website is often in the nature of a 'multimedia' work, which might contain graphics, photographs, (even video) and programming (for instance, JavaScript) from many sources other than the programmer who actually wrote the Hypertext Markup Language (HTML)[337] code which the website basically consists of. This question is discussed below.

326. Not only the user of copyrighted material, but also the provider thereof, is subject to statutory restrictions. The latter have been set out in the ECT Act,[338] in Chapter XI thereof. In order to be considered an online service provider (OSP) for purposes of the act, one has to provide 'information system services' and the latter is, in turn, defined as 'a system for generating, sending, receiving, storing, displaying or otherwise processing data messages (which system) includes the Internet'.[339] The act provides for certain liability limitations if an OSP is a member of the representative body mentioned in section 71 of the act and if it has adopted and implemented the official code of conduct of that body. According to section 71(1) the Minister of Communications may, by notice in the Government Gazette (GG), recognize such a body for purposes of section 72.[340]

327. Another aspect of copyright particular to websites is the matter of source code. By making use of the 'View' command, the casual website viewer can easily read (and copy) the code which underlies the web page(s). This might be HTML, but nowadays might also include XML,[341] XBRL,[342] Java (whether in the form of Java code itself, applets or JavaScript) or any other programming language used in the creation of websites, such as C++. A South African commentator[343] has the following to say on the matter of the protection of source code:

> From a copyright perspective, the source code is protected as a computer program as well as a form of literary work, and any diagrams that may form part thereof are protected as artistic works. Accordingly, the unauthorized reproduction, public performance or adaptation of the source code in a web site constitutes copyright infringement. The owner of a web site must ensure that in the agreement with the web site developer, provision is made for the source code, as well as any intellectual property therein, to be transferred to the owner of the web site.

328. The author also addresses the problem where a specialist website developer maintains the site and, therefore, has full access to, and control of, the source code. He recommends that the website owner and the website developer enter into

---

337. HTML, still the program which has created the heart of the present Internet website system.
338. Act 25 of 2002.
339. Section 72 of the Act.
340. *See* Van der Merwe et al., *ICT Law* (2022), 346ff for further references in this regard.
341. 'Xtensible Markup Language', an interesting development which is dealt with elsewhere in this work.
342. Xtensible Business Reporting Language', a variation for trade and business reporting.
343. Buys (ed.), *Cyberlaw@SA II* (2004), 10.

a contract of escrow,[344] whereby the source code would be placed into safekeeping with a trustworthy third party, such as a reputable financial institution or other company specializing in escrow.

329. Another useful recommendation by the same author is that website owners should always assert copyright in the material that is featured on the website. This should be done in strong terms, such as a copyright warning that would inform people accessing the site that the material on the site is subject to copyright and, therefore, not available for appropriation by users without the permission of the website owner.[345]

330. In the end, South Africa would be well advised to follow international practice with regard to the copyright in websites, because it may be frozen out of international e-commerce and web services if it chooses to follow an idiosyncratic route that is not compatible with the legal systems of its trading partners. A similar situation might obtain because the South African legislature has decided to protect copyright in computer programs by means of a sui generis right,[346] instead of making it part of the category of literary work as the Geneva Council has recommended. In fact, before this amendment, a South African pioneering case[347] had decided that copyright exists in computer programs as a sub-category of literary works.

II. Linking and Caching: The Position of the ISP

331. Another aspect of Internet copyright that has attracted comment from South Africa is when an online web page contains a hypertext link to another site that might possibly be copyrighted. In his work *Cyberlaw*,[348] author Julien Hofman explains that one is impaled on the horns of a dilemma in this regard:

332. It would certainly be possible to treat linking without permission as a breach of copyright or as a breach of the author's moral rights or as passing off. But to require permission for every link would be to deprive the web of much of its flexibility and potential for growth.

333. Hofman suggests that 'the rights of the copyholder should give way to the general good'. This means, in practice, that a mere linking to other sites without permission should not constitute an infringement of copyright.

344. A contract of safekeeping by a third party.
345. Buys (ed.), *Cyberlaw@SA* (2004), 11.
346. By means of an amendment to the Copyright Act 51 of 1977.
347. *Northern Office MicroComputers v. Rosenstein* 1981 (4) SA 123 (C).
348. J. Hofman, *Cyberlaw* (Ampersand Press, 1999), 92.

334. In addition to linking, 'framing' also presents problems with regard to Internet traffic. According to a recent source, the latter practice presents a more controversial problem than the first.[349] The process is described as follows:
Framing is the practice of including large parts from another's website in one's own in such a way that the other parts look as if they are part of one's website.[350]

335. This process, of course, entails making a copy of the controversial part every time a third party visits the framer's website. This might not only involve an infringement of copyright but even of trademark.

336. Closely related to the above two procedures, 'caching' consists of storing copies of downloaded web material for later access.[351] The procedure may take place in one or more of the following ways:

(a) mirror caching, where the service provider stores possible downloads on a separate server in order to speed up future access to that particular information;
(b) web caching, mostly used by ISPs, in order to speed up future access to certain websites;
(c) proxy caching, similar to a), but used on an ordinary local area network (LAN) computer network;
(d) user caching, the user makes own copies of pages accessed during a particular Internet session in order to facilitate future access.

III. Moral Rights

337. Even though South Africa has strong links to the continent of Europe by means of its common law (the Roman-Dutch law), the law of copyright has been completely codified by means of the South African Copyright Act.[352] For this reason the 'moral right' of the author exists only in theory and the holders of copyright have no remedy outside of the four corners of the South African Copyright Act.

349. *See* Van der Merwe et al., *ICT Law* (2022), 324-330 and a discussion of the (overseas) case law cited there.
350. *Ibid.*
351. Van der Merwe et al., *ICT Law* (2016), 260 ff.
352. Act 98 of 1978.

Chapter 5. The Legal Protection of Software

§1. Multimedia and Games

338. Private computers have undergone a transformation from business-like read-only machines (with green text on a black background), to an instrument that is starting to threaten established modes of entertainment such as the cinema. The 'multimedia' element refers to the fact that the latest machines store and play back digitized 'chunks' of media, whether it be graphics, sound, animation, or multimedia encyclopaedias. In fact, the entire concept of an encyclopaedia (digital or printed) is beginning to sound slightly dated in the light of 'always up to date' knowledge bases such as Google. The problem with the quality of the latter type of knowledge, however, lies in the fact that everyone may publish controversial opinions on the Web without these being tested by editorial expertise. The input of an experienced publishing editor (as with printed media) is therefore of the greatest importance.

339. As has been pointed out,[353] this multimedia nature of modern computer media makes irrelevant the rigid classification by the South African Copyright Act of the different types[354] of copyrighted material. In fact, the classification is more than useless; it has become an active hindrance to properly delimiting the rights of copyright holders and users, respectively. Thus, one multimedia work might contain all or many of the categories, which are 'literary or musical works', 'artistic works', 'cinematographic films',[355] 'sound recordings', 'broadcasts', 'program-carrying signals', 'published editions', and 'computer programs'. The last was a later addition by means of a statutory amendment of the Copyright Act.[356] If one wishes to distribute parts of such a program one might need to contact many different holders of copyright, if they had not assigned their rights to an administration body.

340. Because of their great commercial importance, computer games probably constitute the greatest test for copyright. The South African case of *Golden China TV Game Centre v. Nintendo Co. Ltd* [357] has already been briefly mentioned.[358] Although one would not want to quarrel with the deserved lot of the unsympathetic infringers in this case, the theoretical grounding of the decision does leave one with a sense of unease. In a Belgian decision, it was found that Musical Instrument Digital Interface (MIDI)[359] sound files have to be protected in the same category as computer files, because the former are also digital. South Africa has again decided to

353. In para. 84 *supra*.
354. As set out in ss 5–11B of the South African Copyright Act.
355. Which has to be broadly interpreted so as to include videotapes, CD-ROM's, DVDs and nowadays even content downloadable from the Internet.
356. Section. 11B was inserted by s. 10 of the Copyright Amendment Act, Act 125 of 1992.
357. 1997 1 SA 405 (E).
358. *See supra*.
359. A music file in digital format.

follow its own route as far as copyright is concerned and this makes it more difficult to compete in international e-commerce.

§2. Computer Programs: The 'Fair Use' or 'Fair Dealing' Problem

341. The international copyright battle between publishers on one side and libraries and users on the other continues.[360] In South Africa the Copyright Act[361] provided that copyright in the category of 'literary works' shall not be infringed by any fair dealing with that work: '(a) for the purposes of research or private study by, or the personal or private use of the person using the work'.

342. This is an important right in the context of research institutions such as universities. Therefore, it is quite worrying that this right has not been granted with regard to computer programs by the amending Act mentioned above.[362]

343. Commentary on the amendment has been mixed. In an article entitled 'Protection of Computer Programs by Copyright in South Africa', O.H. Dean had the following comment:

> that computer programs, having been fitted out in tailor-made clothing under the Copyright Act, are now adequately protected by the South African law and that the basis has been laid for this form of intellectual product to develop and thrive in South Africa.[363]

344. All comment have not been so favourable. In an article by Pistorius and Visser entitled 'The Copyright Amendment Act 125 of 1992 and Computer Programs: A Preliminary Overview',[364] they point out that by leaving the well-known expedient of protecting computer programs as a literary work and creating its own category, is 'clearly a minority one'. This also entails that the final format of the work will have to be protected sui generis, while preliminary stages of the program, such as flow charts, will still have to be protected under the category of literary works.

345. There is, of course, an easy solution to this problem: scrap the outmoded categorization of the different types of copyrighted works and work with one (multimedia) protected object. So much more, in that South African users have been subjected to legislation that addresses the circumvention of technological measures that have not been designed for copyright protection, but have now been applied to copyright protection.[365]

---

360. *See also supra* for the introductory remarks on fair dealing in general.
361. Act 98 of 1978 s. 12. *See also* in general Van der Merwe et al., *ICT Law* (2022) 359-364..
362. *See* n1 to para. 87 *supra*.
363. *Stellenbosch Law Review* (1995): 87ff.
364. Coenraad Visser, *SA Mercantile Law Journal* 11 (1992): 346ff.
365. For instance, by trying to apply patent-like protection measures to areas traditionally protected by copyright..

Chapter 6. Legal Protection of Databases

346. This represents a comparatively recent, but much-needed development of copyright in South Africa. Living in the information age, the most important assets of companies (and even individuals) consist of the data and information that they keep stored on the CD-ROMs, hard drives, and memory sticks of their computers. Nowadays a safe backup is usually held off-site on the centralized backup computer of a 'cloud' service provider.

347. Pistorius and Visser have criticized the 1992 amendments to the South African Copyright Act[366] for not providing specific copyright protection to databases.[367] In a later lecture note, Pistorius alleges that 'Like new technologies of the past, databases have caught the world's intellectual property system napping'.[368] Both the European Union and the US were in the same position but moved quickly to address this shortfall when the financial worth of databases, and the information contained in them, became clear.

348. In a 1997 amendment to the South African Copyright Act, the definition of 'literary work' in section 1 of the act was widened to encompass 'tables and compilations of data stored or embodied in a computer or a medium used in conjunction with a computer'. This broadening of the South African concept of literary work is to be welcomed, especially because by including media used in conjunction with computers, all kinds of peripheral devices will be included. These could include the digital audio tape (DAT) tape drives on which a daily backup of data is made by many businesses and stored off the premises in compliance with the requirements of insurance companies.

349. In a following case, the copyright protection of a South African database has received judicial scrutiny. This case was *Metro Polis T/A Transactive (Pty) Ltd v. Naidoo T/A African Products*.[369] Metro Polis had been producing the *Auto Data Digest* that contained the specifications of motor vehicles for sale in South Africa. The defendant, Naidoo, had been requested to act as database developer for Metro Polis and, in this capacity, had gained access to all the data, in electronic format. After Naidoo's financial quote in this regard was finally rejected, however, he not only failed to destroy the data but also produced a competing publication. After Metro Polis instituted legal action, the court held that it had successfully established copyright in the data and that Naidoo had wrongfully infringed upon this copyright.[370]

---

366. Act 98 of 1978.
367. In Coenraad Visser, *SA Mercantile Law Journal* 4 (1992), 346ff.
368. Unisa course LML 4810: Legal Aspects of Electronic Commerce.
369. 759 JOC (T).
370. *See* further Buys (ed.), *Cyberlaw@SA* (2004), 15, in this regard.

350. The ECT Act[371] has devoted an entire section of the act to 'critical databases'. The latter term is defined in the definition section of the act[372] as follows: 'a collection of critical data in electronic form from which it may be accessed, reproduced or extracted'.

351. The same section also defines 'critical data' as follows: 'data that is declared by the minister in terms of section 53 to be of importance for the protection of the national security of the republic or the economic and social well-being of its citizens'.

352. Upon such determination having been made, the minister has certain powers that may be exercised by publication in the GG. These relate to the registration and procedures with regard to this type of database,[373] certain minimum standards to be maintained with regard to the management and protection of critical databases,[374] restrictions on the disclosure of information,[375] as well as a right of inspection (or audit) of the critical database administrator by the Director General of the Department.[376]

371. Act 25 of 2002.
372. Section 1 of the Act.
373. Section 54 of the Act.
374. Section 55 of the Act.
375. Section 56 of the Act
376. Section 57 of the Act.

Chapter 7. Protection of Internet Domain Names[377]

§1. LOCAL IMPLEMENTATION

353. Besides introducing the regulation of domain names in general, the ECT Act[378] has also made provision of another innovation, namely Alternative Dispute Resolution (ADR) with regard to domain names. Thus, section 69 provides for regulations to be made in this regard, with due regard to international precedent. A .za Domain Name Authority (Zadna) has been provided for to adjudicate disputes, once the regulations have been passed.

354. The subject matter of this type of regulation is then prescribed[379] as follows:

(2) The regulations may prescribe –

procedures for the resolution of certain types of disputes determined in the regulations and which relate to a domain name registration;
the role which the Authority must fulfil in administering the dispute-resolution procedure;
the appointment, role, and function of dispute-resolution adjudicators;
the procedure and rules which must be followed in adjudicating disputes;
unlawful actions or activities in respect of domain names, distinguishing between criminal and civil liability;
measures to prevent unlawful actions or activities with respect to domain names;
the manner, costs of and time within which a determination must be made;
the implementation of determinations made in terms of the dispute-resolution procedure;
the limitation of liability of registrars and registries for implementing a determination; and
the enforcement and publication of determinations.

355. These regulations were promulgated by the government during November 2006.[380] The regulations spell out the procedures to be followed in the event of a complaint being lodged on the grounds set out in the regulations. These complaints have been adjudicated upon by Zadna's own decision-making body, an accredited alternative dispute-resolution service provider. To date, two such dispute-resolution

377. *See* in general Van der Merwe et al., *ICT Law* (2022) 274ff on management of the domain name system..
378. Act 25 of 2002. *See also* Van der Merwe et al., *ICT Law* (2022), 285ff for a further discussion of ADR in a digital context.
379. Apparently as a *numerus clausus*?
380. By GN R1166 published in GG 29405 of 22 Nov. 2006. *See* right holder, the master licensee (franchise holder) etc. For a critical discussion *see* E. Hunter '*An evaluation of selected aspects of the Alternative Dispute Resolution*', SA Merc LJ (2007): 165–185.

bodies have been accredited, namely the Arbitration Federation of South Africa (AFSA) and the South African Institute of Intellectual Property Lay (SAIIPL). A number of the SAIIPL's decisions are described in Van der Merwe et al., *ICT Law* (2022).[381]

§2. Other Types of Dispute Resolution in the IT Sector

356. Besides the above-mentioned, statutory, modes of dispute resolution, some other start-up operators have started to advertise their services in this regard, specifically as ADR agents with regard to disputes that do not necessarily relate to domain names.

§3. Online Dispute Resolution

357. This heading differs from the previous one in that the method used for solving a dispute in any area of the law[382] may now be by means of IT technology. In a South African work on IT and the law, namely *Cyberlaw@SA III*,[383] a section has been devoted to the topic of online dispute resolution. This is now carried out by means of regulations in terms of the corresponding section of the ECT Act.

358. A number of technological issues may also delay (or even prevent) the adoption of electronic ADR in South Africa for the immediate future. These are, *inter alia*, the lack of face-to-face discourse and personal interaction as well as security issues that might arise from the lack of confidential communications. Response times and other technological issues might also 'throw a spanner into the works'. For an instructive overview of the need for such a system, but also a realistic assessment of the impediments delaying it, *see* the Master of Laws (LLM) treatise of Nabawanuka entitled 'Development of a Self Enforceable Online Arbitration System is the Key to Effective Online Dispute Resolution'.[384]

---

381. Van der Merwe et al., *ICT Law* (2022), 289-296 and also available at <www.domaindisputes.co.za/content.php>. These cases turn mostly on proof of entitlement to the disputed right, marks which are confusingly similar and abusive registrations (made in bad faith).
382. Thus not necessarily confined to an IT-related topic.
383. Snail and Papadopoulos (eds.) *Cyberlaw@SA* (2012), 214 ff.
384. LLM (UCT) (2006).

Part V. Cybersecurity Law

§1. Cybersecurity: An Introduction

359. This field basically entails a careful evaluation of the security risks that a given user's ICT assets, resources and activities are exposed to and includes the formulation and quantification of countermeasures, as well as the prediction of the effectiveness of such countermeasures.[385] These should involve the compilation and putting into effect of business continuity plans if a security breach should bypass the above countermeasures. Formerly known as 'disaster recovery' this field has now (perhaps less alarmingly) come to be known as business continuity.

360. In this regard a world-wide standard has been accepted and this is known as ISO 17799. It focuses on multiple facets such as physical and environmental security, system and access control as well as on personnel security. It has often been found that the last-mentioned (human) element forms the weakest link in an otherwise effective security system. The present author has found one of the most useful sources on the entire topic of ICT security to be the chapter by Maeson Maherry entitled 'Security in e-commerce'.[386] He takes great pains to point out that the real threat to an organization's information does not lie in 'hordes of evil hackers lurking on the Internet just waiting to attack and deface your Web site'.[387] He argues that the real danger 'lies within' in that many organizations have not yet learned the value that should be placed on protecting their data.

§2. The Proper Investigation of ICT Security Breaches

361. An important part of any investigation into a suspected instance of computer crime is constituted by the field of computer forensics.[388] 'Forensics' might be described as 'the following of certain acknowledged standards during the investigation of and presentation of evidence against the accused, which procedure might persuade the court to admit such evidence and give due and proper weight to it.'

385. Van der Merwe et al., *ICT Law* (2022), 77.
386. In a chapter by that name in the work *E-commerce in Practice* (2004) by Carstens and Lucouw.
387. *Supra* 69.
388. The word 'forensics' actually comes from the Latin *forum* meaning 'court'.

362. This gathering and analysis of information concerning an instance of possible computer crime is a complex process that entails determining the nature of the crime, the degree of technical expertise involved in committing it, as well as the history of this type of crime in the particular environment surrounding the present instance. It should also involve liaising with personnel as well as with management to investigate any relevant personal connections between any of the role players.

363. It is interesting to note that a previous draft of the present Cybercrime Act[389] tried to introduce many cybersecurity provisions including the formation of a permanent 'Cybersecurity Hub'. However, the present Act has now dropped almost all security provisions concentrating in the main on creating a slew of new cyber-offences as well as a number of accompanying criminal procedure provisions.

389. Act 19 of 2020.

Part VI. Cybercrime

Chapter 1. Application of International and Regional Agreements

364. One of the most laudable initiatives in this regard has been the Council of Europe (CE)'s Convention on Cyber-crime. As stated in the work *Information and Communications Technology Law*[390] 'One of the major problems with cyber-crime is precisely its international nature, which gives rise to problems of jurisdiction, incompatible procedural-law systems and so forth.'

365. The first part of this convention requires signatories to ensure that a number of offences are prohibited nationally. South African common law already takes care of many of these such as computer-related forgery and fraud, but the statutory equivalent could now be charged in the alternative. Others are covered by statute, for instance the illegal interception of, or interference with, the transmission of data. Finally treaty countries have to criminalize certain copyright-related offences. The South African legislature has ensured that South Africa would comply with all of these requirements by means of various pieces of legislation, including the recently enacted Computer Crime Act.[391]

366. In the second part of the convention, procedural matters are set out including a warning to set sufficient safeguards for human rights to be protected adequately. On this point some incompatibility is possible between the accusatorial system followed by South Africa (and the Anglo-American world) as against the inquisitorial system ubiquitous in most continental countries.

367. In Part Three the convention deals with matters such as the international cooperation in the investigation and prosecution of criminal offences. Unfortunately, South Africa has not yet brought this country up to date as far as procedure and international relations are concerned.

390. Van der Merwe et al., (2022) 117ff.
391. Act 19 of 2020.

Chapter 2. Specific Computer Crimes

§1. Introduction

368. Many of the crimes that people are charged with in South Africa today originate from the South African common law (*see* above, Historical Background to the South African Legal System as part of the General Background to this entire volume). Thus, crimes such as murder, rape, theft, malicious injury to property, and housebreaking all originate from the Roman-Dutch law. One characteristic of all these historical crimes that presents a major problem for IT crime is the fact that they only dealt with tangibles (something physical that one could touch). This has caused a great amount of uncertainty in the South African legal system and the perception arose that the common law would not be able to cope with IT crime.

369. This will soon become apparent when discussing some typical IT crimes. For instance, the crime of theft in Roman-Dutch law is only possible with regard to a physical tangible object. This has created numerous problems with regard to the theft of money. Whereas South African common law has had no problems with the theft of physical notes or coins, it is a different story when dealing with 'money' as an abstract concept. In the IT world, this is typically what would occur when some clever hacker has siphoned 'money' from your electronic bank account.[392]

§2. Common-Law Crimes in South Africa in Relation to IT

I. Theft

370. 'Theft' has been defined as the 'unlawful contrectatio (taking), with intent to steal, of something capable of being stolen'. The real problem, especially in the ICT law context, is whether information, as an intangible matter, is capable of being stolen.

371. By means of some imaginative interpretation (by creative lawyers) of the concept of money as part of a trust relationship, the South African courts have managed to reach the point where a sum of money, as an abstract concept, can now be stolen. In the case of *R v. Milne and Erleigh*,[393] the Appellate Division decided that one could steal the rights arising out of possession of a cheque. In *R v. Manuel*,[394] the court held as follows: '(U)nder our modern system of banking and paying by cheque or kindred process the question of ownership of specific coins no longer arises where resort to that system is made.'

392. This comes down to the fact that the purchaser had to know that relevant writing existed on the package, and to know that this writing bore relation to his contract with the licensor. This bears the further implication that the person offering the document should have done what was reasonably sufficient expected in terms of commercial practice.
393. 1951 (1) SA 791 (A).
394. 1953 (4) 523 (A).

372. In *R v. Scoulides*,[395] reference was made to both cases cited in paragraph *349* above by Schreiner, J.A.:

> These cases establish that ownership at different points of time of the individual notes or coins is not important in deciding whether a theft of them has been committed. What is decisive is whether the sum of money, considered as such and not made up of individual notes and coins, which the accused person took or consumed was already his to deal with as he pleased for his own benefit, or whether it was really held in trust for the complainant."

373. If it had been held as part of a so-called trust relationship the sum of money was therefore susceptible to the crime of theft. Notwithstanding the fact that this type of crime has been called 'theft by conversion', it is really more akin to the crime of fraud than to the crime of theft. Even though a number of courts have dealt with the same kind of legal object, none of them have moved beyond a kind of 'trust relationship – theft by conversion' kind of scenario. It would, therefore, seem that our unknown hacker, siphoning off 'money' from an electronic bank account would not be guilty of theft unless he or she had had some kind of prior trust relationship with the victim.

374. The common-law crime of theft, which has served the South African legal system reasonably well for a number of centuries, is therefore not very suitable for combating IT crime in South Africa.

II. Fraud

375. Thus far, the term 'fraud' has been used without properly defining it. A working definition could be 'the obtaining of some real or potential advantage by means of an unlawful intentional misrepresentation'.

376. Because of the wide definition of the element of 'advantage' in the crime of fraud, it is clear that much computer-based trickery would found possible charges of common-law fraud. Nevertheless, one particular IT-based scenario again produces more than its share of problems.

377. Take the situation, for instance, where the perpetrator had obtained the cash card or credit card of the victim (John Smith), has worked out a way of getting around the password protection (not that impossible!) and now represents himself as John Smith to an ATM. The poor machine is 'taken in' by this misrepresentation, duly dispenses the money and the perpetrator makes off with his ill-gotten gains.

378. What crime should the perpetrator be charged with? Fraud would seem to be the obvious crime, except for one problem. Can one make a 'misrepresentation' to a machine, in the sense that the machine is 'deceived' by this? It is true that

395. 1956 (2) SA 388 (A) at 394 F-G.

human bank clerks will do a control check of the operation of the machine at the end of the day, but by that time the 'advantage' has already been 'obtained' and cannot be said to have been caused by the misrepresentation. It would seem that the common-law crime of fraud is also not always the answer to IT crime.

III. Malicious Damage to Property

379. This may be defined as the unlawful intentional causation of damage to the property of someone else.

380. In *S v. Howard*,[396] one of the first applications of the old common-law crime to the modern techniques of 'hacking', the so-called Edgars Hacker was charged with malicious injury to property for having released a virulent virus program on the computer system of his employer. This was done as 'revenge' for labour-related matters. He was convicted and sentenced to five years imprisonment. What is interesting about this case is that it took place before the passing and promulgation of the ECT Act – in other words, he was convicted in terms of common law.

381. As readers would probably have gathered by now, the central problem is whether the element of 'property' may be extended to something as intangible as a computer system. In the above case, the perpetrator did not get away, despite of the focus on tangibles by the South African common law. Because he had brought down a nationwide computer system, including peripherals like the point of sale system, the court felt that this was tangible enough. In the alternative, the court decided that the law was ripe for an extension in this regard. The common-law crime of malicious injury to property might thus still be the answer to the creation and distribution of computer viruses.

IV. Housebreaking

382. This crime may be defined as the unlawful breaking and entering of premises with intent to commit some further offence. Because this is a 'double-barrel' offence, prosecutors often speak of 'breaking and entering' – the displacement of some part of a door or a window (breaking) as well as slipping through the opening thus created (entering).

383. The definition cited in the previous paragraph has led to some ludicrous situations. If a very thin burglar can slip through a window that is already partly open, without displacing or moving any part of it, he or she has not committed the 'breaking' part of the offence and will at most be guilty of trespassing. On the other

396. In the Johannesburg commercial regional court in the unreported case no. 41/256/02. *See also* the case-discussion by M Watney in 2005 TSAR.

hand, if he or she comes down the chimney without displacing anything, this will still be considered as breaking (perhaps because the chimney has to be kept open for the arrival of Father Christmas).

384. Applying the common-law crime of housebreaking to the computer hacker, the problem arises whether one's computer system can be seen as 'premises'. This seems unlikely, as courts have always interpreted to be something 'in the nature of a house', even though they have included caravans, outbuildings and such in the definition. Even the crime of trespassing has traditionally been limited to 'premises'.

385. It seems, therefore, that the common-law offence of housebreaking (and even the statutory offence of trespassing) will not address adequately the problem of hacking into computer systems.

V. Other Forms of Cybercrime

386. Perhaps because the focus in criminalizing actions relating to e-commerce is so much on protecting objects with monetary value, other forms of cybercrime have been neglected. In the following few paragraphs, some crimes which go to protect the morals (really to protect people against themselves) will also be discussed. Within a work of this nature, with limited scope, the author will simply focus on crimes relating to pornography and crimes relating to gambling.

387. As far as *pornography* is concerned, the crime is dealt with in terms of the Films and Publications Act.[397] This was amended in 1999 to specifically cope with pornography on the Internet, and a 2003 amendment increased the maximum prison terms for this offence from five to ten years. In *S v . Rawlinson,*[398] a regional court case in Durban, the accused was convicted on a majority of the charges relating to child pornography. However, he was acquitted on one count, because the 'victim' concerned testified that she had only used that particular computer to play Solitaire. The Act's definition of 'publication' was extended in 1999 by a statutory amendment so as to also include 'any message or communication, including a visual representation, placed on any distributed network including but not limited to, the Internet'.

388. As far as the other 'sin', namely *gambling* is concerned,[399] another court had to deal with the gambling licence of Casino Enterprises in Swaziland. Because everything was organized from, and manned by, people in this country neighbouring South Africa, it was argued that the casino did not need a South African gambling licence. In *Casino Enterprises vs the Gauteng Gambling Board, the National*

397. Act 65 of 1996. *See also ICT Law* (2022) by Van der Merwe et al., at 86-87 and 613-615.
398. Case no. 041/3019/05, decided in September 2007.
399. *See ICT Law* by Van der Merwe et al., *ICT Law* (2022), at 87ff.

Gambling Board and the Minister Trade and Industry[400] the court held, however, that Swazi legislation could not apply extra-territorially, and since South African citizens were taking part in the gambling by means of the Internet, this could not be allowed without a licence from the corresponding Gauteng body.

§3. Reaction by the Legislature

I. Introduction

389. It was clear that the situation described above could not be allowed to continue. With the coming of electronic commerce, a reliable legal infrastructure was needed to provide the necessary trust and reliability. South Africa became one of the first countries in Africa to address these problems by means of the ECT Act.[401]

II. Crimes Created by the ECT Act

390. The following number of paragraphs will deal with the crimes created by the legislature in 2002. In general, these provisions have been greeted with acclaim because they seemed to cover a major gap in the arsenal of South African crimes. Constituted by sections 86 and 87 of older Act, these offences have now been repealed by the more specialized Cybercrime Act.[402]

391. The Interception and Monitoring Act has since been repealed by the Regulation of Interception of Communications and Provision of Communication-Related Information Act,[403] which itself creates a number of new offences.[404]

However, to return to the recent Cybercrime Act from the Department of Justice and Correctional Services. Chapter 1 is entirely devoted to definitions, in most instances differing to a marked degree from those offered in the ECT Act.[405] For instance, the term 'article' is very widely defined to mean:

> any (a) data, (b) computer program, (c) computer data storage medium or (d) computer system which is (i) either concerned or connected with the commission or suspected commission, (ii) may afford evidence of such commission or suspected commission, (iii) is intended to be be used, or on reasonable grounds believed to be used in the commission or intended commission of such offence, whether in terms of the laws of the Republic or in terms of laws of foreign states.

---

400. SCA [2011] ZASCA 155; [2011] 4 All SA 573 (SCA).
401. Act 25 of 2002.
402. Act 19 of 2020.
403. Act 70 of 2002.
404. *See* p69 among others.
405. All definitions are contained in s. 1 of the Act, as is the case with almost all South African legislation.

In contrast to the ECT Act, the Cybercrime Act is brave enough to attempt a definition of the term "computer", namely as "any electronic programmable device used, whether by itself or as part of a computer system".[406] "Computer system" is defined in turn as "any device or equipment, or part thereof" which is able to "perform predetermined arithmetic, logical, routing, processing or storage operations in accordance with set instruction and includes any data, computer program or computer data storage medium that are related to, connected with or used with such a device." In turn a "computer data storage medium" is then defined as "any device from which data or a computer program is capable of being reproduced or on which data or a computer program is capable of being stored by a computer system, irrespective of whether the device is physically attached to or connected with a computer system". The legislator should be complimented, in the present author's opinion, for conceptually separating the data from the computer program and from the computer data storage medium. This is also the conceptual separation in which XBRL-programming has driven programmers to think and forced (reluctant!) lawyers to reason. A "computer program" means "data representing instructions or statements that, when executed in a computer system, caused the computer system to perform a function".

392. In the opinion of the present author one of the most important definitions is that of a 'computer system', namely as:

(a) one computer; or
(b) two or more inter-connected or related computers which allows these inter-connected or related computers to –

exchange data or any other function with each other; or
exchange data or any other function with another computer or a computer system.

393. The term 'data message' is preserved in the new Act, but clarified by removing the restrictions imposed by the ECT Act as far as the requirements of 'voice' and 'a stored record' are concerned. The precise meaning of 'electronic communications service' and 'electronic communications service provider' have also received a timely elucidation.

394. The 'output of a computer program' has also been penetratingly analysed as '(a) data or output of the data; (b) computer program; or (c) instructions, generated by the computer program.' On the other hand, an 'output of data' simply means 'having data displayed or in any other manner'.

406. *See ICT Law* by Van der Merwe et al., at 70ff.

395. Also important is the definition of 'traffic data' as relating to 'the route which communication will take. It means data relating to communication indicating the communication's origin, destination, route, format, time, data, size, duration or type of the underlying service.'

396. Chapter 1 of the new Cybercrimes Act covers Definitions, but Chapter 2 is entitled 'Cybercrimes, Malicious Communications, Sentencing and Orders protecting Complainants from the Harmful Effect of Malicious Communications'. Part 1, dealing with 'Cybercrimes', comprises the corresponding sections in the previous ECT Act, but with significant and important changes and extensions. Section 2(1) of the new Act criminalizes certain actions with regard to either a computer or a computer storage medium. The unlawful and intentional 'access' to such a system is declared to be criminal. In turn, 'access' is defined to include both the 'use of ' and 'storage on' of a computer system or storage medium, respectively.

397. On the other hand, section 3 prohibits the interception of data. 'Interception' with the latter being widely defined so as to include even the electromagnetic emissions from a computer containing such data. In turn, subsection 4(1) criminalizes the use of, or even the mere possession of, 'any software or hardware instrument' with the purpose of committing actions prohibited in sections 2, 3, 5, 6 or 7 of the present Act. In turn, subsection 4(2) provides an extensive definition of 'instrument' so as to include even 'a password, access code or similar data'.

398. Section 5 simply prohibits the unlawful interference with either data or a computer program, while section 6 extends this prohibition to a computer storage medium or system. The latter prohibition adds an interesting value worthy of protection, namely confidentiality. Section 7 prohibits the possession of any password or other form of access code in order to contravene the prohibitions in this part of the Act.

399. As with the ECT Act, a number of common law offences are given statutory equivalents, namely in section 8 (Cyber-Fraud), section 9 (Forgery and Uttering) and section 10 (Cyber-extortion). The methods in committing these offences are now described in greater detail. Section 11 introduces the new concept of 'Cyber Offences' which attack 'restricted computer systems' specifically. The latter concept is defined as 'any data, computer program, computer data storage medium or computer system under the control of or for the exclusive use of a financial institution or an organ of state, including a court which is protected by security measures against unauthorized access or use.'

400. One of the most problematic innovations has been the creation of a new statutory offence by section 12 of the Act. This criminalizes the so-called Theft of Incorporeal Property. This clause is likely to confuse the Criminal Law in the present case with the fields of Patent Law and the Law of Copyright. In Roman-Dutch law the crime of theft was restricted to tangible goods alone,

401. In turn, Part II of Chapter 2 of the Cybercrimes Act now deals with 'Malicious Communications'. Here section 13 contains a number of definitions pertinent to the crimes dealt with in this part. Thus 'damage to property' means 'damage to any corporeal or incorporeal property'. Again, this is a radical deviation from the Roman-Dutch law definition of this crime - see the similar procedure followed with regard to definition of theft, discussed in the previous paragraph. The term 'disclose' in respect of a data message means sending a data message to another person and to 'store' means 'storing a data message on an electronic network where it may be viewed and downloaded' or 'sent or made available on an electronic communications network'.

402. Part III then deals with all forms of inchoate (or incomplete) crimes, such as attempt and/or conspiring and with participation in the crime of another.]

403. Chapter 3 of Part III covers jurisdiction and deals with the modern modes of 'long-arm jurisdiction' that have become almost a necessity in the days of the World Wide Web.

404. Finally, even though the Act deals with the basics, and does so quite well, it deserves special mention because of the way it focuses on both the externals (consisting of the hardware involved) but also on the real value contained in the data that needs to be protected.

III. Other Statutory Crimes: The RIC Act

405. Mention has already been made of the Regulation of Interception of Communications Act 70 of 2002. After this Act (RIC Act for short) was signed into force, a number of criminal provisions have come into effect. The statutory penalties for these will not be as restrained as in the case of ECT Act, discussed above.

406. Thus subsection 51(1)(b) of the RIC Act provides as follows:

> Any person who is convicted of an offence referred to in – para. (a) or in sec. 49(1) or 54 is liable to a fine not exceeding R2,000,000 or to imprisonment for a period not exceeding 10 years.

407. Section 49 deals with:

> any person who intentionally intercepts or attempts to intercept or authorizes or procures any other person to intercept or attempt to intercept, at any place in the Republic, any communication in the course of its occurrence or transmission.

408. Section 54 deals with the tampering with telecommunications equipment.

409. One may well wonder about the necessity of legislation such as this when the ECT Act, in section 87(1) already prohibits the interception of communications, albeit with the threat of a mere two years of imprisonment as the maximum penalty. One's sense of proportion is shocked upon learning that this same activity is now threatened by a fine of ZAR 2 million and imprisonment of ten years as the maximum penalty. Perhaps the ECT Act should have had a chance to prove its merits first.

410. The RIC Act gets worse. Subsection 51(2)(b)(i)(bb) provides for a fine of ZAR 5 million for legal persons (companies). This draconian punishment is for postal service providers who fail to obey an interception direction or who disclose any information that they are not at liberty to disclose.

411. The RIC Act is also controversial for appearing to take control over internal communications away from the employer, unless the latter has managed to persuade each employee to sign a release. Thus, in section 6, which deals with 'Interception of indirect communication in connection with carrying on of business', subsection 6(2) states the following:

> A person may only intercept an indirect communication in terms of subsection (1) –
>
> (a) if such interception is effected by, or with the express or implied consent of, the system controller;
> (b) for purposes of –
>   (i) monitoring or keeping a record of indirect communications; or in order to establish the existence of facts; for purposes of investigating or detecting the unauthorized use of that telecommunications system; or
>   where that is undertaken in order to secure, or as an inherent part of, the effective operations of that system; or
>   (ii) monitoring indirect communications made to a confidential voice-telephony counselling or support service which is free of charge, other than the cost, if any, of making a telephone call, and operated in such a way that users thereof may remain anonymous, if they so choose;
> (c) if the telecommunications system concerned is provided for use wholly or partly in connection with that business; and
> (d) if the system controller has made all reasonable efforts to inform in advance a person who intends to use the telecommunications system concerned, that indirect communications transmitted by means thereof may be intercepted or if such indirect communication is intercepted with the express or implied consent of the person who uses that telecommunications system.

412. The piece of legislation described in the previous paragraph constitutes a truly strange section. From the 'and' following on subparagraph (c), it would appear that the four subsections are cumulative, in other words that the conditions described in all four sections all have to be present at the same time before such a communication may be intercepted. If this is so, then subsection 6(2)(b)(i)(bb) which deals with 'detecting unauthorized use' would clash with subsection 6(2)(d) which requires the 'express or implied consent of the person who uses that telecommunications system'. Perhaps the resolution of these two opposites might lie in the fact that the user has to give a general consent to monitoring for unauthorized use up front and then willingly take the risk that his unauthorized communications might be 'caught out' in a specific instance.

413. Also strange is the fact that the access of the employee to anonymous counselling services may be monitored (again with his or her consent). Would this be so that the boss can fire his or her 'unstable' employee afterwards?

414. Section 6 has attracted a lot of excited debate as to whether employers should have their employees all sign releases so that the conditions in subsection (d) may be complied with. Of course, even if this happens, the employee would still be entitled to rely on the protection built into the other subsections.

415. An 'indirect communication' is defined in section 1 of the RIC Act as follows:

> the transfer of information, including a message or any part of a message, whether in the form of –
>
> > speech, music or other sounds;
> > data;
> > text;
> > visual images, whether animated or not;
> > signals; or
> > radio frequency spectrum; or
> > in any other form or combination of forms;
> > that is transmitted in whole or in part by means of a postal service or a telecommunications system."

416. In contrast to this, a 'direct communication' is almost always constituted by direct, face-to-face communication.

417. Looking at the definition of 'indirect communication' it would seem to include anything that may be 'sent' via the Internet, a telephone system or even by means of the post. The fact that physical mail is included separates the application of the RIC Act from that of the ECT Act, which deals with 'data' and 'data messages' which would always be in an electronic format.

418. The RIC Act also contains a number of criminal law provisions, many of them characterized by the unexpectedly high penalty clauses by which they are fortified. In a recent edition of the work entitled *ICT Law* [407] some of the more onerous provisions are criticized. The Act both bestows and controls regulatory powers, particularly in relation to the transmission and interception of data. One of its most controversial provisions has proven to be section 44 read with section 51, which deal with record-keeping by any person who 'sells or in any manner provides' any cell phone or SIM card to any other person. Casual buyers and sellers or someone 'taking over' a phone that is no longer wanted by the former owner are unlikely to comply with such onerous requirements. Section 51(1) contains a complete list of the criminal provisions of the Act and lists crime which may be committed by 'any person' in general, and by postal service providers, telecommunications service providers and/or decryption key holders, or by the employees of any of the above.

IV. Promotion of Access to Information Act 2 of 2000

419. The criminal provisions of this PROATIA Act (as it has come to be known) are quite straightforward in comparison to those of the RIC Act.

420. Section 90 of the PROATIA Act provides as follows:

> A person who with intent to deny a right of access in terms of this Act –
> destroys, damages or alters a record; or
> conceals a record; or
> falsifies a record or makes a false record;
> commits an offence and is liable on conviction to a fine or to imprisonment for a period not exceeding two years.

421. It is to be welcomed that the PROATIA Act has been as restrained as the ECT Act in imposing criminal sanctions. It is also very necessary to have this provision since it protects the right to information, which is bestowed on each South African citizen by our Constitution.

422. The right to information, mentioned in the previous paragraph, is guaranteed by section 32 of the South African Constitution, Act 108 of 1996:

(1) Everyone has the right of access to any information held by the state; and any information that is held by another person and that is required for the exercise or protection of any rights.
(2) National legislation must be enacted to give effect to this right; and may provide for reasonable measures to alleviate the administrative and financial burden on the state.

---

407. By Van der Merwe et al., *ICT Law* (2016): especially at 82ff.

423. Even though the PROATIA Act was specifically enacted to give effect to subsection 32(2) of the Constitution, as quoted above, after fifteen years there remains considerable doubt as to whether this (rather bureaucratic) piece of legislation has succeeded in its goal.

Chapter 3. Criminal Procedural Aspects

§1. Introduction

424. Whereas the criminal law, treated above, constitutes part of substantive law, the law of criminal procedure is part of adjective law.

425. Substantive law basically sets out what one's rights and duties are in real life. The Ten Commandments of Moses would constitute a good example of substantive law. Criminal law and private law are examples of fields of substantive law. By contrast, adjective (or procedural) law tells one what your rights and duties are relating to court procedure. Examples would be the law of criminal procedure, the law of civil procedure, and the law of evidence.

426. The rest of this section will thus be devoted to adjective law, in other words, the law of criminal procedure as well as the law of evidence.

§2. Historical Background

427. Even though the common law for criminal law was the Roman-Dutch law, as was explained above, this is not the case with criminal procedure. Before 1652, the people of South Africa were governed by tribal legal systems. Great emphasis was placed on the authority of the chief, who had final legislative, executive, and judicial authority. He (or she in a few cases) also determined the procedure to be followed, who could speak when, etc. This was an important responsibility, because the whole tribe assembled for the hearing and each member was entitled to ask questions, make comments, and demand explanations. This gave the chief a good feel for the background to the case and he or she could act on the popular feeling on the matter.

428. The above is an example of inquisitorial procedure, in which the judge takes an active role in proceedings. By contrast, the procedure followed in British courts is much more of an accusatorial procedure, which means that the judge acts as an impartial referee. We will hear more about the accusatorial procedure further on.

429. The fact that the Roman-Dutch law is still the common law for a great part of South African law, stems from the fact that the Cape of Good Hope used to be a Dutch colony with courts schooled in the Dutch way of criminal procedure. In fact, these courts were known as *Landdroste en Heemraden*, with the *Heemraad* being related to the jury system. Nevertheless, the courts were still, broadly speaking, inquisitorial.

430. In 1806, however, the Cape was finally conquered by the British, and the judiciary began to be populated by British judges and magistrates. Because these two groups of worthy gentlemen knew nothing of Dutch procedure in courts, they simply applied the British system of criminal procedure (while striving to keep the substantive Roman-Dutch law going, however). The procedure was very much accusatorial, with the judge sitting aloof, simply controlling the other actors in court such as the prosecutor, the witnesses, the accused, and his defence attorney. This position was well put in one decision, where the judge was warned against 'entering the arena, and having his eyes clouded by the dust of the conflict'. Because juries were often used, a strict system of admissibility of evidence arose. This will be discussed under the law of evidence below, but it is important to realize that many evidential rules are based on the type of criminal procedure.

§3. Legislative Developments

431. Today, the South African system of Criminal Procedure takes the British system as its common law. In fact, the South African Criminal Procedure Act,[408] contains some so-called residuary provisions – a 'residue' from the British system. We will be meeting some of these residuary clauses in the later section on evidence. South Africa became a republic and left the British Commonwealth on 31 May 1961. These clauses try to preserve the common law by referring to 'the law as it was on 30 May 1961', in other words, on the last day that South Africa was part of the British Commonwealth and, therefore, amenable to British rules of evidence and procedure.

432. In a (much earlier) version of the Criminal Procedure Act, these provisions spoke of the law applied by 'His Majesty's Courts of Record at Westminster' and later of the law applied by the 'Supreme Court of Judicature'. These references obviously meant the law of criminal procedure as applied in the English courts. It was probably to protect the sensibilities of patriotic South Africans that these offending clauses were later changed to the more neutral: 'the law which applied on the 30 May 1961', because at least the 'hated' English courts were no longer mentioned by name.

433. Being of a 'Before Computer (BC)'-vintage, the South African Criminal Procedure Act has struggled to deal with the latest cyber developments. Fortunately, a section of the new Cybercrimes Act[409] has shed some light on the interface between criminal procedure and IT technology. This is discussed in greater detail in one of the latest works on the subject of the general relationship between computers and law.[410]

408. Act 51 of 1977.
409. Act 19 of 2020.
410. *See* the Chapter on Cybercrime *ICT Law* (2022) Van der Merwe et al., pp 97ff.

§4. Analysis of the South African Criminal Procedure Act

I. Background to the Act

434. This is the latest incarnation of an Act that has remained the same in basic structure for many years now.[411] Very little has been done to bring it up-to-date as far as IT-related needs are concerned. As has been shown above, the Act is based on the British system of evidence and criminal procedure. It has replaced the common law entirely and regulates the entire field of criminal procedure for South Africa. The only exception to its general provisions would be in the event that a specific statute prescribes procedural rules to govern a specific situation, covered by that statute. The exception would also be in line with the rule of interpretation *generalia non specialibus derogant* (general provisions do not derogate from specific ones).

II. Search and Seizure

435. The police have to find enough evidence to prove every element of an offence in order to found a conviction for that offence. If any such evidence is found, the police have to 'seize' (confiscate) it. The Criminal Procedure Act specifically prescribes the procedure to be followed during these two activities. Following the correct procedure is even more important since the South African Constitution[412] has come into being.

436. Section 14 of the Constitution guarantees each citizen the right to privacy, in the following terms:

> Everyone has the right to privacy, which includes the right not to have –
>
> their person or home searched;
> their property searched;
> their possessions searched;
> the privacy of their communications infringed.

437. The question of the privacy of communications as well the protection of privacy in general will be discussed under Part VII below. Looking at section 14 of the Constitution, which has just been cited under paragraph 421 above, the question may arise whether the Criminal Procedure Act should not be declared invalid and unconstitutional when it gives the police the right to do precisely what the Constitution is trying to prevent, namely the unwarranted search of a suspect's person, home, property, or possessions. Fortunately, the right to privacy is not absolute; otherwise, criminals would have welcomed the Constitution with open arms. The Constitution also contains section 36, which limits constitutional rights, as follows:

411. Act 51 of 1977.
412. Act 108 of 1996.

(1) The rights in the Bill of Rights may be limited only in terms of law of general application to the extent that the limitation is reasonable and justifiable in an open and democratic society based on human dignity, equality, and freedom, taking into account all relevant factors, including –

the nature of the rights;
the importance of the purpose of the limitation;
the nature and extent of the limitation;
the relation between the limitation and its purpose; and
less restrictive means to achieve the purpose.

438. Each section of the Criminal Procedure Act that allows the police to infringe upon these privacy rights thus has to be tested against all these factors. Here (b) – the importance of the purpose of the limitation, is probably vital. It will always have to be shown that no other means to obtain the evidence existed. Section 20 of the Criminal Procedure Act provides as follows:

The State may, in accordance with the provisions of this Chapter, seize anything (in this Chapter referred to as an article) –

which is concerned in or is on reasonable grounds believed to be concerned in the commission or suspected commission of an offence, whether within the Republic or elsewhere;
which may afford evidence of the commission or suspected commission of an offence, whether within the Republic or elsewhere; or
which is intended to be used or is on reasonable grounds believed to be intended to be used in the commission of an offence.

439. The fact that the article cited in the previous paragraph speaks of 'anything' would tend to include even information. The execution of the warrant is made easier by the fact that the intangible information would usually be contained in a tangible object such as a computer, CD-ROMs, memory sticks, etc. Because sections 33(3)(a) and 300(4) of the Criminal Procedure Act deal with the disposal of money which has been confiscated, it is obvious that money is included among the articles which may be confiscated in terms of section 20.Much argument might be spent on the supposedly objective standard of 'reasonable grounds'. Again, it is too easy for the magistrate to subjectively see him or herself as the reasonable person, able to discern reasonable grounds ex post facto.[413] Section 21 of the Criminal Procedure Act requires that the article to be seized must be described clearly in a search warrant. In the case of pure information, this will probably be impossible and the tangible 'containers' of information should be specified. Often an entire computer is removed from the premises of the suspect because of the ease with which incriminating evidence might be deleted from the machine.

413. The famous armchair critic being wise *after the event*.

440. On the other hand, the machine cannot be kept in quarantine until the case is brought before the court, because the suspect obviously needs to carry on with his or her business or whichever purpose he or she had been using the computer for. For this reason, a 'dump' of all information on the computer onto a tape drive or some other voluminous medium should be done and the computer be returned to the suspect. Three copies are usually made – one to be sealed and kept in a secure environment until the court date. Another is to be used by the prosecution to do tests on and to scour for relevant evidence. The third is to be returned to the suspect so that he or she may prepare the defence case. This gives the prosecution a 'time slice' to work with. It also makes it impossible to prove offences that have been happening over time, unless several 'time slices' are taken.

441. A certain technological development almost put paid to the evidential value of the sealed original because it has always been presented that its integrity is above suspicion. A piece of computer code, called (rather aptly) 'Tombstone', was apparently able to self-destruct upon a given event, say a certain date, or because the computer has not been left on enough during a certain time period. This could happen notwithstanding the fact that the medium has been under control of the prosecution (or a neutral third party) for the entire period between seizure and the trial date. The only antidote seems to have been to make a 'hard copy' (a printout on paper) which will have to be marked and dated before independent witnesses. Nowadays 'Tombstone' code has lost its sinister connotation and is simply used to indicate where former code has been removed from a computer program.

442. Section 30(3) of the Criminal Procedure Act determines that the police have to keep any exhibits in their custody until the case can be brought before the court. Section 33 determines that the exhibit has to be transferred to the clerk of the court where the criminal proceedings are about to be instituted. Because of these 'movements' of the exhibit, it is of the utmost importance that a 'trail of evidence' be laid by a witness to show that the article has not been interfered with between the seizure and the evidence presented. For this purpose, the exhibit usually has to be identified by means of a distinguishing mark and/or number. If the original state of the exhibit is disputed, a series of witnesses may have to be called to guarantee the 'route' of the exhibit from the moment of seizure, its journey to the police station or other place where it was stored, its state while in storage, and finally its journey to court. Again, it seems to be almost impossible to keep a trail of evidence with electronic data, unless the data has been encrypted immediately after seizure and decrypted immediately before being used as evidence before court. This would probably require expert evidence from a person skilled in cryptography[414] and even better, evidence from the actual expert involved in encrypting and decrypting the code concerned.

---

414. *See* Part I, Ch. 8 *supra*, on the regulation of cryptography in South Africa.

§5. STATUTORY UPDATES TO CRIMINAL PROCEDURE

443. A valid question that might arise is whether, and to what extent, the new Cybercrimes Act of 2020 has had an impact upon criminal procedure.[415] In the first place, the copious references in the ECT Act[416] to a new body of 'Cyber-inspectors' have been removed completely.

444. Furthermore, copious use is made of the existing Criminal Procedure Act.[417] Section 28 of the Cybercrimes Act deals with the search for, access to, or seizure of certain articles. Section 29, in turn, enables these actions to be performed in terms of a valid search warrant and section 30 covers the oral application for such a warrant or the amendment of such. Section 31 authorizes such actions with the consent of someone who has the lawful authority to do so. Section 32 authorizes the same, but without a search warrant. Once the suspect has been arrested, section 33 prescribes the next actions following thereon. Section 34 authorizes the assistance of such a police official or investigator and section 35 criminalizes the obstruction of the person carrying out the arrest and authorizes the overcoming of such resistance. Section 36 warns that these powers of arrest need to be carried out in a 'decent and orderly manner and with due regard to the rights of other persons. Section 37 prohibits wrongful search, access or seizure and places a restriction on the use of an instrument, device, password or mere information to gain access to any information in an unlawful manner.

445. Section 38 forbids the rendering of any false information, section 39 forbids the disclosure of certain types of information and section 40 covers the interception of indirect communications and the obtaining of real-time communication-related information.

446. The next four sections deal with so-called data directions. Thus section 41 deals with the 'expedited' preservation of a data direction, section 42 with the 'ordinary' preservation of the same and section 43 with an oral application for a preservation of evidence direction. Section 44 covers the disclosure of a data direction and the search for, access to and seizure of articles subject to preservation. Finally, section 45 covers the obtaining and use of data that is publicly available or receiving data from a person who is in possession of that data.

415. See *ICT Law* (2022) by Van der Merwe et al., at 98ff.
416. Act 25 of 2002, now partially repealed by the later Cybercrimes Act.
417. Act 51 of 1977 s 27.

Part VII. Contractual and Non-contractual Liability

Chapter 1. Computers and the Law of Contract

§1. Introduction

447. In the first edition of the first work on computer law in South Africa, *Computers and the Law*,[418] contracts were dealt with at the hand of a checklist, which was more useful with the then current system of contracting for bespoke, turnkey,[419] mainframe computer systems. These systems were made up of huge mainframe computers that had to be installed permanently in a specially prepared location and had to be serviced exclusively by the original provider. Security was easy because of physical access control (which is much easier than controlling electronic access) and the fact that the computer was only connected to in-house dumb terminals.[420] This means that much of what was written in the first edition is now of little value. One set of rules still hold good, however. It is likely that both hardware and software will be sold by means of standard form contracts and the skeleton of this contract could form a nice basis for negotiation. According to the first edition, the characteristics of standard form contracts were as follows.

448. Ideally, all such contracts should have an introduction, setting out the purpose of the contract and identifying the principal parties thereto. The purpose should indicate the type of legal relationship that is being created, for instance, whether a lease or licence is intended, but should also describe the subject matter accurately and completely. In the case of many computers, the only solution to the latter problem is to append a complete technical specification as a schedule to the contract.

449. In the second place, the contract should set out the buyer's obligations, which usually consists of paying the contract price (possibly staggered) also according to an appended schedule. The buyer may also be obliged to cooperate with the vendor on topics such as site preparation, testing, etc.

418. Van der Merwe, *Computers and the Law* (Juta, 1986), at 60ff.
419. Like a car, a complete self-contained system is delivered – it is ready to start at the turn of a key (turnkey).
420. A dumb terminal means that it has no processing power in itself but has to receive it from the network. The so-called 'network' computer (or 'thin client') is simply a modern reincarnation hereof.

450. The third category consists of two series of obligations by the vendor, one being to meet the contractual deadline for delivery, installation, testing, etc., and the other being to give the required technical support in the form of training, maintenance, updating of software, etc. It is quite important to marry any deadlines to easily determinable dates, for instance, a given period following an 'effective date', which is set by the signing of the contract.

451. Fourth, an unrelated number of topics are usually included, often dealing with matters such as ownership, the passing of risk, insurance, and confidentiality.

452. Nowadays, even the most powerful servers are movable machines which are often also usable as personal computers, except that they spend most (or all) of their 'lives' hooked up to the umbilical cord of a network and acting as servers. Even though Intranet[421] also existed in mainframe days, they were linked to dumb terminals (*see* above) that had no independent processing power. Today, personal computers serve as the terminals, often in the shape of laptops or even phones and pads and they are quite capable of working independently from the network, provided the proper software is installed.[422] Software is generally sold over the counter as commercial packages and no longer has to be painstakingly programmed in-house. The world is facing threats, technical and legal, from problems (such as hackers) which were unheard of in 1986. All this necessitates a fresh look at the question of computer contracts.

453. An overview of hardware contracts will be followed by a more extensive analysis of software contracts, followed in turn by the differing application areas for the spectrum of contracting. In part IV, the contracts that form the heart of electronic commerce will be analysed.

§2. HARDWARE CONTRACTS

454. Computers may be sold, leased, or rented. A maintenance contract would probably be part of the main contract but separate arrangements are often made. According to Karin Alheit, in her doctoral thesis entitled *Issues of Liability Arising from the Use of Expert Systems*,[423] argued that contractual terms may be express[424] or implied. She described implied terms as follows:

> Implied terms describe the unexpressed provisions of a contract which are imported by law (ex lege) without regard to the intention of the parties, or they may consist of terms implied by the facts or circumstances of the case (ex consensu). The ex lege implied terms of a contract differ according to the form of

421. A LAN within a particular organization.
422. Ignoring for arguments' sake the possibility of the so-called network computer which will almost be a reversion to the old 'dumb terminal'.
423. (1997) Unisa at 93ff.
424. Express terms usually come about expressly by the use of unambiguous words in the contract.

contract entered into. Such terms are in fact one of the naturalia of the contract which apply automatically if they are not excluded.

455. Alheit also distinguishes between *essentialia* (prescribed terms of law that have to form part of a contract to give it a specific character), *naturalia* (the default terms unless excluded by the parties), and *incidentalia* (matters which the parties have freely negotiated among themselves without being prescribed to by law).[425]

456. With a contract of sale, some of the *naturalia* are the obligation of the seller to deliver the goods, to prevent the buyer from being evicted from his title to the goods and to accept responsibility for latent defects in the goods. The last gives rise to the so-called aedilitian[426] actions. These actions permit the buyer of a product with latent defects to cancel the contract and ask for his money back (with the *actio redhibitoria*) or at least claim a reduction in the selling price (with the *actio quanti minoris*). They will only apply where the seller publicly claims to possess certain skills and/or expertise with relation to the product and the buyer, therefore, relied upon these in entering into the transaction. Almost any computer dealer will fall within this category.

457. Something as technologically complex as a computer might easily show defects in use which were not apparent beforehand and, therefore, sellers of computer hardware are keen to exclude this kind of liability by means of exemption clauses (typical *incidentalia*) and, in exchange, to provide a maintenance clause. According to Alheit these exemption clauses 'are used to empower contractants in a strong bargaining position to exploit co-contractants in a weaker position'. South Africa does now have a Consumer Protection Act.[427]

458. In South Africa, most computer hardware is bought from dealers who exclude common-law warranties but make available a maintenance contract in its stead, either rendering this service themselves ('carry in' or 'on site') or making use of an outsourced third party specializing in computer maintenance. Care should be taken with this complex of contracting parties, bearing in mind that one is dealing with different parties in giving up and gaining rights. For instance, you give up your common-law rights as against the seller, who in turn offers you maintenance, which he again has to contract for with a third party on your behalf.

425. K. Alheit, *Issues of Liability Arising from the Use of Expert Systems* (1997) (unpublished LL.D. thesis 1997 Pretoria, University of South Africa) at 94.
426. Named after the *aediles curules*, magistrates in Roman times who had to keep a watchful eye over commercial activities.
427. Act 68 of 2008.

§3. SOFTWARE CONTRACTS

459. Again, standard form contracts are used (often from overseas principals not willing to negotiate individual clauses) but now the type of contract changes.[428] Instead of buying or leasing as in the case of hardware, software is mostly licensed. This originates from the days when copyright protection of software was reasonably uncertain, and the software author decided to rather entrust his brainchild to the protection offered by the law of contract. According to Alheit, a licensing agreement is an innominate contract unknown to our common law.[429] This has the implication that it has no *naturalia* that will determine the scope of the agreement. A typical example might read as follows:

> Customer is granted a personal, non-transferable and non-exclusive license to use each X Disk Product. The license does not include the right to sublicense, assign, copy, reproduce, distribute, prepare derivative products of the X Disk Products, or alter the provided content on the flexible disk in any way.

460. 'Non-exclusive' means that the product is also being licensed to other users and 'personal' and 'non-transferable' means that the user may not allow anyone else to use the program. To get around this severe restriction (legally) the so-called site-licensing contract is used. This simply means a kind of mass-licence that enables an entire institution (such as the University of South Africa) to buy one (very expensive) copy of a software package and then make it available over the network to as many users as the site-licence provides for.

461. In a licensing agreement, it will usually be important for the licensor to retain ownership of any backup copies that the licensee may be allowed to make. If ownership does pass, it may be stipulated that the extra copies have to be destroyed by the new 'owner' as soon as his licence expires.

462. Other than with the old mainframe computers, when purchasing a 'programmed computer' for the company was a major decision, solemnized with handshakes and photographs of the contracting parties, most modern software is sold over the counter or even electronically over the Internet. This is a result of so-called unbundling, in the sense that the customer no longer needs to buy the software and the hardware bundled together.

463. When a typical mass-marketed software is sold over the counter, two contracts are actually involved. The first is between the shop owner who received the money and hands over the package and between him and the customer the nature of the contract is still one of sale. However, a second type of contract used to come into being shortly afterwards when the user wants to tear the cellophane of 'his' or 'her' software package but was greeted by the following words:

---

428. *See* in general on the formation of software contracts Van der Merwe et al., *ICT Law* (2008), 147ff.

429. K. Alheit, *Issues of Liability Arising from the Use of Expert Systems* (1997) (unpublished LL.D. thesis 1997 Pretoria, University of South Africa) at 86.

> READ THIS PAGE CAREFULLY NOW, before opening the sealed diskette package. YOU AGREE THAT BY OPENING THE SEALED DISKETTE PACKAGE YOU HAVE SHOWN AGREEMENT TO THE LICENCE TERMS BY YOU AND ANY OTHER USER OF THIS SOFTWARE. (If you don't wish to enter this agreement, return this package with the sealed diskette package unopened to your dealer with your receipt for a full refund.)

464. This constituted the so-called shrink-wrap[430] agreement, which saw the act of tearing the transparent cellophane wrapping off the software package as acceptance of the licensing terms. Van der Merwe et al. emphasize how the 'click-wrap' package has by now replaced the 'shrink-wrap' type of contract and has become an important tool in modern business. [431]

465. Alheit draws an analogy with the UK 'ticket' cases where the customer receives a 'ticket', not supposed to be signed, which bears on its back the terms between the customer and seller. In this case, the customer is held liable even if he denies being aware of the terms printed on the back of the ticket. The equivalent problem on the Internet arises when a potential customer is presented with a screen full of legalese and has to indicate his assent to all conditions with a mouse-click (a so-called click-wrap contract) in a certain spot, usually labelled 'I agree'. If he does not, the program does not proceed. This leaves one with the difficult legal situation where the customer has 'purchased' the package from the software seller but only afterwards learns about some licensing condition with which she cannot agree. What exactly would her legal position be in this case?

466. To fully understand the problem, one has to understand that the typical software purchasing situation consists of two transactions.[432] The first is a contract of sale between the dealer and the customer, the second a licensing contract between the copyright holder and the customer. If the customer baulks at the licensing contract, he then also has to cancel the contract of sale by handing the package back to the dealer for a refund of the purchase price. The situation becomes problematical when he takes the package home, installs it, and finds that he has to click on the screen to accept the licensing conditions. I suspect that most users do this almost automatically as part of the installation procedure without applying their minds to the conditions, which might fill two or three screens with densely scrolling text. Even worse, the mouse-click is often done by the friend or employee with computer expertise, who is doing the installation on behalf of the purchaser.

467. Another matter vital to licensing contracts is whether computer software should be seen as goods or services. This question will obviously affect the legal remedies of the contractants. As mentioned above, the sale of goods with latent defects gives rise to the aedilitian remedies under the proper circumstances, whereas

---

430. Named after the process which tightly stretches transparent cellophane over the box containing the software.
431. *See* Van der Merwe et al., *ICT Law* (2008), 166 on these.
432. Also illustrated by the two stages in the purchase of the shrink-wrap package described above.

the rendering of poor service can only lead to cancellation of the contract and a claim for damages. Alheit examines the situation in the US and in the UK.[433] According to the US law, a program that is mass produced and marketed is likely to be classified as a 'product' and would, therefore, be covered by the phrase 'sale of goods' in Article 2 of the Uniform Commercial Code (UCC), and fall under that regime. On the other hand, a program that has been specially written (custom made) for one specific user would be classified as a 'service' rendered by the programmer and the legal situation would be covered by common law, since a 'sale of goods' did not take place. English courts try to analyse the substance of the contract to see whether something which has been produced beforehand is sold or whether the contract calls for the future exercising of skill and labour. In the former case, goods have been sold and in the latter, services have been contracted for.

468. An interesting sub-theme is whether the fact that a program is fixed on a disc or other material medium can convert the object of the contract into goods and, therefore, into a contract of sale (and not services).

469. It has been argued that because the value of the carrier medium (disks, tapes, etc.) is so insignificant compared to the total value of the program, these media cannot affect the nature of the transaction. This argument is something along the lines of *de minimis* non *curat lex.*[434] On the other hand, authors such as Tapper[435] and Reed:[436]

> find these arguments unconvincing and also irreconcilable with the treatment of books and works of art. A book is indisputably tangible property which constitutes 'goods' in legal terms, notwithstanding the fact that its major value lies in the writing, and not in the book. Therefore, software embodied in a physical medium is a good or product.[437]

§4. Different Types of Contracts

470. Even with regard to one product (services), many different types of contract may be obtained. The same applies to goods where acquisition may take a number of different forms. The following section will explore the ramifications of the different types of contract, measured by their very nature, not by the type of product that they govern (goods or services). It should also be borne in mind that each of these different types of contract may have different default terms implied *ex lege* and thus have different *naturalia* (*see* above).

---

433. K. Alheit, *Issues of Liability Arising from the Use of Expert Systems* (1997) (unpublished LL.D. thesis 1997 Pretoria, University of South Africa) at 109ff.
434. 'The law does not concern itself with trivialities'.
435. *Computer Law* 4th ed., (London: Longman, 1989) at 181.
436. *Computer Law* (Oxford: Blackstone, 1996) at 43.
437. Cited by Alheit, *Issues of Liability Arising from the Use of Expert Systems* (1997) (unpublished LL.D. thesis 1997 Pretoria, University of South Africa) at 111.

I. Contracts for the Purchase and Sale of Goods or Services

471. In this case, 'the seller undertakes to deliver possession of a thing in return for the purchaser's undertaking to pay a sum of money'.[438] *Essentialia* would, therefore, be agreement on the nature of the thing sold and agreement on the price. Otherwise, as is the case with the Law of Things, the thing may be corporeal or incorporeal. The *naturalia* would include the liability of the seller for latent defects (as discussed above) and an implied warranty to the buyer against eviction. As mentioned above, these *naturalia* constitute the default position and these consequences might be varied or excluded by means of *incidentalia* (special agreements between the parties for this particular contract). Software being what it is, no product will ever be completely free of bugs (latent program defects), but the courts have decreed that software need only be as functional as could reasonably be expected from such a product.[439] Alheit also deals with liability of the seller (or supplier) as follows:

472. Liability for consequential and other damage is almost always excluded by the seller because of the high risk of potentially large claims as a result of defective software. Liability of the supplier is also mostly limited to the remedying of defects or the replacement of defective software or the purchase price.[440]

473. According to Alheit, the seller's main duty *ex lege* is to deliver the software in accordance with the stipulations of the contract (which used to include a long list of specifications and testing procedures in the old mainframe days). If he has guaranteed the absence of defects or the presence of certain good qualities in the software and the software fails to live up to these warranties, a breach of contract (warranty) is committed and direct or consequential damages may be claimed with the *actio empti.*[441] A 'manufacturer' of the product (which in the case of software would be the developer), may incur liability in terms of the *actio empti* even if no warranties had been given and she was ignorant of the existence of the defects. A seller who is unaware of the defect will be liable 'where he publicly professes to have attributes of skill and expert knowledge in relation to the kind of goods sold'.[442] Most modern software shops such as 'The Incredible Connection' and 'The Computer Superstore' would probably qualify on this count.

474. In the case of delivery of something defective, without the seller having given any warranties or having made any representations of the nature described above, he might still be liable in terms of the aedilitian actions, the *actio redhibitoria* and the *actio quanti minoris* mentioned above. The first gives the buyer the

438. K. Alheit, *Issues of Liability Arising from the Use of Expert Systems* (1997) (unpublished LL.D. thesis 1997 Pretoria, University of South Africa) at 122ff.
439. *Holmdene Brickworks (Pty) Ltd v. Roberts Construction Co* 1977 (3) SA 670 (A) at 683.
440. K. Alheit, *Issues of Liability Arising from the Use of Expert Systems* (1997) (unpublished LL.D. thesis 1997 Pretoria, University of South Africa) at 123.
441. *See* De Wet and van Wyk's *Kontraktereg en Handelsreg* (1992) at 339 and the cases cited there.
442. *Kroonstad Westelike Boere Ko-operatiewe Vereniging Bpk v. Botha and Another* 1964 (3) SA 561 (A) at 571.

opportunity to resign from the contract and reclaim the purchase price, whereas the latter keeps the contract intact but makes provision for a reduction in purchase price. According to Alheit this *ex lege* liability for latent defects may be excluded by agreement, and the sale will then be *voetstoots* (or 'as is'). She cites the following requirements for the aedilitian actions:

(1) a defect in the thing that renders it completely unfit or less fit for the purpose for which it was bought – the test is objective and the purpose for which it was bought can mean its normal use or a special use contemplated by the parties;
(2) the defect must not be negligible;
(3) the defect must not be apparent upon inspection by an average person – the test is objective;
(4) the defect must have existed at the time of the sale; and
(5) the purchaser must not have been aware of the defect – the onus of proof is on the purchaser.

II. Contracts for Lease or Rental

475. A contract of letting and hiring of things (lease) originates from the *locatio conductio rei* in Roman times. According to Alheit it is 'an agreement whereby one party (the lessor) undertakes to grant the other party (the lessee) the temporary use and enjoyment of a thing in return for the latter's undertaking to pay the rent in money'. The essentialia are the above-mentioned agreements with the *ius utendi fruendi*,[443] the rent and the temporary transfer of the rented thing. The *naturalia* coming from the common law include protection against latent defects and a guarantee that the property will be enjoyed freely (*commodus usus*). The main duty of the lessor is to deliver the thing let to the lessee in the above manner and the main duty of the lessee is regular payment of the rent and care of the thing let.

III. Contracts with Regard to the Provision of Services

476. This is a contract for the letting and hiring of work, originating from the *locatio conductio operis* in Roman times. (This has to be distinguished from the normal contract of employment[444] where the employee works permanently in the service of the employer.) The essentialia of the *locatio conductio operis* are that a piece of work is let out by the lessor to the lessee who agrees to the work in return for remuneration. The remuneration is usually calculated in money but does not necessarily have to be in this format.[445] To pay this and to see that the lessee is not out of pocket, are the main obligations of the employer. On the other hand, the main

443. Literally 'the right of using and enjoying'.
444. Known in Roman law as *locatio conduction operarum.*
445. It might be a share in the profits of a company or the produce of a farm – *see* De Wet and Van Wyk at 384.

obligation of the employee is to finish the piecework that he has been contracted to do. Bespoke or custom-made software usually fall under this heading. According to Alheit, the *locatio conductio operis* carries an implied warranty that the work will be done in a proper manner and that the materials used will be of good quality and suitable for the particular purposes.[446] The common-law liability for latent defects may be validly excluded, as with a contract for purchase and sale.

IV. Contracts for Professional Services

477. Related to the previous topic is that of professional liability. This may arise from delict or contract, and only the latter is dealt with here. It refers to the liability that might be incurred by a person engaged in a profession, trade, or calling that demands special knowledge and skill.[447] Negligence is, therefore, judged according to a higher standard because more can be expected from an expert than from a layperson. The *ex lege* duties imposed by this kind of contract (categorized by Alheit as one of mandate) on the professional are to perform the task, to obey instructions, to exercise care and diligence, to advise and impart information, to account and to show good faith. If the professional does not meet the higher standards expected of a professional, she might be found negligent and the client might claim damages.

478. According to Alheit, the exclusion of liability would not be invalid but the general rule is that professional persons of integrity should not resort to this mechanism.[448] What hurts the feelings of many computer programmers is that their field has not yet been seen as a truly professional area of endeavour. When this happens, it would also build in a degree of protection for the consumer.

V. Licensing Agreements

479. Many of the issues arising out this type of agreement have already been discussed above, for instance that it is an innominate contract with no applicable *naturalia* and that software is often obtained by a combination of a contract of sale (between the dealer and the end user) and a licensing contract (between the copyright holder and the end user). According to Alheit,[449] the way in which software is transferred onto the user's computer system should not really make a difference to the nature of the transaction taking place.

446. K. Alheit, *Issues of Liability Arising from the Use of Expert Systems* (1997) (unpublished LL.D. thesis 1997 Pretoria, University of South Africa) at 128.
447. *Ibid.*, at 131 and the sources quoted there.
448. *Ibid.*, at 133 and the sources quoted there.
449. *Ibid.*, at 129.

480. Alheit also refuses to accept the argument by Sieg Eiselen[450] and Maré[451] that licensing might serve as a contract of acquisition as well as the way of regulating the use of copyrighted material. The reader will recall her argument above that two contracts are usually involved in each transaction, namely one of sale by the dealer to the customer, and a licensing contract by the copyright holder licensing the use of the software to the customer. Alheit's argument runs as follows:

> To view the 'licensing' of software also as a manner of acquisition apart from sale, lease or the provision of services, is in my opinion, to negate the essence of the transaction taking place when software is acquired, which is that the user is put in the possession of a specific manifestation of the software as owner, lessor or the recipient of a service which includes the acquisition of the product, in exactly the same way as a book or tape or any other copyrighted product. Even the fact that software may be directly transferred electronically or installed on to the user's computer system, makes no difference to the nature of the transaction taking place. Depending on the nature of the transaction, the latter products are purchased, hired or acquired by way of a locatio conductio operis. To state in the case of a book for example that the purchaser of the book is not the owner thereof is absurd. The only difference between the latter products and software, to my mind, lies in the prescription of the use of the copyrighted material: in the case of software such use is much more narrowly defined than in the case of books and tapes, but the manifestation of the software remains the object of a sale or lease or whatever the case may be.[452]

481. Alheit then concedes that this matter has not yet been authoritatively decided by the courts and that licensing might still turn out to be a form of acquisition sui generis. I feel that this is another example of the uneasy coexistence of traditional private law with the Law of Intellectual Property. Before information became such an important asset these overlaps could be papered over, but now the strains are beginning to show. It also became manifest in the chapter on copyright above,[453] where the question of whether an independent right of use should still be catered for, even when unauthorized copying has been prohibited, raised equally intricate problems. While the process of copying remained an a priori[454] prerequisite to use (as with paper copies), the two fields could be kept distinct. Once the copying and the use took place simultaneously and inextricably bound up with each other (as with the use of the Internet) the borderlines grew faint. Mention was made of Coenraad Visser's argument that copyright owners must be considered to have

450. G.T.S. Eiselen '*Computer Contracts*' (1996) unpublished memorandum PUCHE 1996. Many of Eiselen's arguments are now encapsulated in Chapter 6 'E-commerce' in Van der Merwe et al *ICT Law* (2022) 161 where electronic contracts are discussed in depth. Particular attention is given to Electronic Data Interchange (EDI) as a manner of contracting electronically and also to the section of the ECT Act, 25 of 2002, dealing with contracts.

451. E. Maré, *Evaluering van kontraktipes by die verskaffing van rekenaarprogrammatuur* (1995) unpublished LL.M. thesis PUCHE.

452. Alheit, *Issues of Liability Arising from the Use of Expert Systems* (1997) (unpublished LL.D. thesis 1997 Pretoria, University of South Africa) at 132.

453. *See supra.*

454. Something which has to take place in time before the subsequent event.

tacitly permitted reproduction if they allow their material to be placed on the Internet. One wonders whether this is an implied licence to make a transient copy, an implied right to use, or both.

§5. CONTRACTS: INCIDENTAL MATTERS IN THE ELECTRONIC FIELD

482. A matter that is of the utmost importance: (a) is proving the terms of a contract; and (b) that the contracting parties have agreed to all these terms. For purposes of proof, it would obviously be much safer to have a contract in writing and signed by the contracting parties. In these days of word processors and e-mail, this is becoming problematical, but technologies such as 'electronic signatures' should make electronic contracts possible. This matter was more fully explored in the Law of Evidence above in Part III, Chapters 3 and 4. Good precautionary practice might be to create one printed out 'original' which is to be signed physically be contracting parties and witnesses.

483. Other matters such as all the different types of remedies and the type and quantum of damages are not that relevant to computer law specifically and a more specialized work on contract should be consulted in this regard. The same goes for specimen contracts – these would have over-filled a publication of the present nature.

I. Legal Status of Electronic Transactions

A. *Introduction*

484. From what has already been explained about the Roman-Dutch law,[455] it is clear that this legal system, as the common law of South Africa, will also govern the law of contract. However, as with certain aspects of criminal law, a number of adjustments might have to be made in order to cover electronic transactions. Even though written contracts are only required in a limited number of instances, which are prescribed by statute,[456] this type of contract by means of the Internet was not anticipated by our common-law forebears.

485. In order to forestall interpretation problems and to encourage electronic commerce in South Africa, the ECT Act,[457] therefore, provided for electronic transactions to be legal provided these comply with its conditions. This aspect is covered under the next heading. It is important to keep in mind, however, that the traditional common law requirements of offer, and acceptance and a meeting of the minds (consensus) will probably remain the essential elements of a contract, even if concluded electronically.

455. *See* Part III, Ch. 2 *supra*, in this regard.
456. For instance, any transaction dealing with the transfer of land has to be in writing.
457. Act 25 of 2002.

B. Electronic Transactions in Terms of the ECT Act

486. Section 22 of the ECT Act provides that an agreement (or contract) will not be without force and effect merely because it was concluded partly, or in whole, by means of 'data messages'.[458] This concept has been defined earlier on in the ECT Act as: 'data generated, sent, received or stored by electronic means and includes voice, where the voice is used in an automated transaction; and a stored record'.[459]

487. It, therefore, seems clear that offer and acceptance, even by electronic means, will suffice for a valid contract. An interesting possibility is raised by the mention of voice, namely that an oral contract, or contract by word of mouth, is now possible with VOIP[460] technology.

488. Section 23 of the ECT Act provides that a data message used in the conclusion or performance of an agreement will be taken to have been sent when it enters an information system outside the control of the originator. This should solve many of the traditional problems with regard to postal contracts as far as the Internet is concerned.

489. Section 24 determines that an expression of intent or other statement will not be without force and effect merely because it is in the form of a data message, or is not evidenced by an electronic signature,[461] but by some other means from which such person's intent or statement can be inferred. section 25(3) also attributes a data message to the originator if it was sent automatically by a pre-programmed information system, unless it is proved that the system did not properly execute its instructions. The wording of this subsection would seem to place a burden of proof on the person alleging such a fault.

490. Finally, section 26 determines that an acknowledgment of receipt of a data message is not necessary to give legal effect to such message.

491. It is to be hoped that these provisions will help to move South Africa into the brave new world of e-commerce, mainly by inspiring confidence in overseas trading partners that full legal effect would be given to their legal online transactions. *See* further on e-commerce the relevant chapter[462] in *ICT Law* [463] for the latest developments in this regard.

---

458. *See* in general Van der Merwe et al., *ICT Law* (2022),. 218ff.
459. All definitions are contained in s. 1 of the Act, as is the case with almost all South African legislation.
460. Voice over Internet Protocol.
461. *See* Part IV, Ch. 3 *infra* in this regard.
462. Chapter 6 on e-commerce by Eiselen.
463. (2022) 218ff. Also use the general index at the back of the book for particular issues.

Chapter 2. Computers and Non-contractual Liability

§1. GENERAL INTRODUCTION

492. This chapter will attempt to clarify the interface between computers and the field of private law, except for the law of contract, which has just been dealt with in Chapter 1, §3 *supra*. Private law is a complex, multi-faceted area of law, and we will concentrate on the following areas. In Chapter 2, §2, The Law of Things, the question of real rights in immaterial goods and the commodification of information will be explored. Chapter 3, §3, The Law of Delict (or *tort* in English legal systems) will explore the borders between contractual and delictual liability at the hand of practical examples. Finally, Chapter 4, §3, III will deal with the liability of ISPs, a group that plays an increasingly pivotal role in the success of e-commerce. Privacy will be dealt with in Part VIII *infra* – an important factor as far as the Internet is concerned, especially when considering e-commerce on this medium.

493. Because the Roman-Dutch law is alive and well in South Africa as far as private law is concerned, the latter is very much a home-grown affair. This means first that comparative law is not that useful in order to solve typical South African problems. Historical research is often more rewarding in South African private law but would obviously have limited value in the area of computer law. In the second place, most of South African private law is formed by the courts interpreting the Roman-Dutch law, and this field is not as regulated by statute as many others. This gives the system an enviable flexibility and ability to adopt change. Whether it is able to cope with computers remains to be seen. Throughout, one should bear in mind that South Africa, since 1994 has been a *Rechtsstaat* (a country governed by law as the ultimate authority) and that we have a Constitution[464] with teeth in order to protect the human rights of the individual. Particularly where technology threatens a personal right, such as privacy for instance, the Constitution might well be called upon to play a role.

494. It seems sad to say but the journey through the world of private law which the reader is about to undertake, leaves one with a sense of a legal system which has not kept pace, especially not with IT-related matters. The Roman-Dutch law has always shown remarkable resilience in adapting to change, but may now have come to the end of the road if it cannot deal with computers and the new information-based wealth of the Information Age. Particularly the law of things has left the field of immaterial things wide open to be (imperfectly) filled by branches of the law of intellectual property, such as copyright, competition law and trade secrets. The question of the commodification of information and digitized property should actually have been the domain of private law. Yet one has some sympathy with the following point of view:

464. Act 108 of 1996.

> Throughout the time I've been groping around cyberspace, an immense, unsolved conundrum has remained at the root of nearly every legal, ethical, governmental, and social vexation to be found in the Virtual World., I refer to the problem of digitised property. The enigma is this: If our property can be infinitely reproduced and instantaneously distributed all over the planet without cost, without our knowledge, without it even leaving our possession, how can we protect it? How are we going to get paid for work we do with our minds? And if we can't get paid, what will assure the continued creation and distribution of such work?[465]

495. The legal IT-author Katsch provides the answer by pointing out that, in contrast to most corporeal possessions, the value of information diminishes rapidly when stored statically and is only valuable if it is ploughed back in the information market. He cites Barlow's examples of sharks that are said to die of suffocation if they stop swimming:

> The same is nearly true of information. Information that isn't moving ceases to exist as anything but potential . . . at least until it is allowed to move again. For this reason, the practice of information hoarding, common in bureaucracies, is an especially wrong-headed artefact of physically based value systems.

496. Again, this would seem to fit in with my personal definition of information as '(desired) items of knowledge, news'; Whereas knowledge can be protected and hidden, information should be a public commodity, in whose waters any citizen can fish for personal knowledge.

497. Katsch also cites Peter Drucker as follows:

> Knowledge is power, which is why people who had it in the past often tried to make a secret of it. In post-capitalism, power comes from transmitting information to make it productive, not from hiding it.[466]

498. Once the true nature and value of information has been addressed by private law, criminal law will breathe a sigh of relief and the law of intellectual property can go back to expressing tangible expressions of ideas. Until that happy moment, all these fields of law will have to continue to develop sui generis models and quasi-rules to patch up the law so that it can at least run, even though backfiring on one cylinder and never knowing when it may break down completely. The law is not quite the vehicle with which to embark upon the rapid journey around the world that the Internet involves. An added complication is constituted by the high expectations that young black students have of the law in South Africa. They do not feel that the Roman-Dutch system is part of their historic background and feel that this should be replaced by something more 'African'. On the other hand, most of the rules of traditional black law have been developed against a rural background

465. John Perry Barlow as cited by Ethan Katsch, *Law in a Digital World* (Oxford, 1995), 223.
466. Katsch, *Law in a Digital World* (1995), at 224.

where courts were held by tribal chiefs and fines paid in head of cattle. The present author is of the opinion that South Africa should do its best to become part of a modern e-commerce world where each of the trading partners respect and cooperate with the legal systems of the other partners.

§2. COMPUTERS AND THE LAW OF THINGS

I. Introduction

499. Being still grounded in the tangible, uncodified world of Roman-Dutch common law, the law of things has experienced a great deal of difficulty in dealing with incorporeal matters, such as electricity, information, and even money in its modern sense. I have first explored these matters in an article that initially was supposed to deal with the theft of information from a criminal law perspective, but I then found that the trail led straight to private law and to the doctrine of subjective rights, imported from continental Europe.

500. The doctrine of subjective rights and their accompanying competencies has first been popularized in South Africa by W.A. Joubert.[467] This long-held foundation of all legal debate from the Afrikaans universities has been overtaken by recent events, specifically because of its insistence that the Law of Things (*Sakereg*) confine its attentions to material, movable things, thus leaving all immaterial things, from electricity to information to be handled by the law of immaterial property. The first such challenge came from the present writer in an article entitled 'Diefstal van Onliggaamlike Sake met Spesifieke Verwysing na Rekenaars'.[468] In this article, I argued that the problem of 'theft of information' was not really a problem of criminal law, but that it had originated from the failure of private law, notably the law of things, to adequately deal with immaterial things. This was followed by Duard Kleyn's contribution to the 1992 edition of *Silberberg and Schoeman's The Law of Property* [469] as well as L.C. Coetzee's 'Die Rol van die Onstoflike Saak in die Sakereg'[470] and finally, an article from Kleyn entitled 'Dogmatiese probleme rakende die rol van onstoflike sake in die sakereg'.[471] Kleyn argues that the concept of 'thing' be extended to 'anything whether corporeal or incorporeal that is of use and or value to man and which is regarded as *in commercio*'.

467. *See* his articles in THRHR 21 (1958): 12ff and 98ff. It is worth noting that Joubert does not like the expression intellectual *property* because this would seem to imply real rights.
468. '*Theft of Immaterial Goods with Specific Reference to Computers*' SACC (1985): 129.
469. (Juta 1992), Ch. 2.
470. '*The Role of the Immaterial Thing in the Law of Things*' (1992 LL.B. treatise University of Pretoria).
471. '*Dogmatical Problems with Regard to the Role of Immaterial Things in the Law of Things*', De Jure (1993): at 1ff.

501. In my own article,[472] I quoted an article by J. Eksteen, who (already in 1984) foresaw the problems that the interfacing between computers and law was likely to lead to:

> The computer is such a novel concept in itself and one so far removed from the contemplation of the founders of our legal system, that the application of the principles framed by them often presents considerable difficulty when seeking to apply them to the behaviour of people using computers.

II. Can Information Be Made the Subject of Real Rights?

502. In pursuing the question whether information may be stolen, I was led to attempt answering the question as to whether information (or other immaterial goods) could be made subject to real rights, such as ownership and possession in terms of the law of things. The answer seemed to be that only corporeal objects could be subject to these rights, although a few anomalies gradually became apparent. Thus in C. G. van der Merwe's work *Sakereg*,[473] he admits that Roman law did distinguish between *res corporales* and *res incorporales*[474] but that he still prefers to confine the law of things to corporeal matters for two reasons. The first is that this facilitates the categorization of the different kinds of subjective rights into four watertight categories, namely real rights, personal rights, personality rights, and immaterial property rights. The second is that a real right should imply direct physical control over the object to which it applies. (To this one might reply that any systematization should be reviewed in the light of new developments that do not fit neatly into existing paradigms – 'back to the drawing board'.) Later on, van der Merwe has to admit that in certain 'exceptional cases', immaterial goods may form the object to a real right,[475] at another juncture he describes similar cases as 'anomalies',[476] and third,[477] he admits that certain incorporeal things may form the object of theft and that legal rules which are 'analogous' to those applicable to corporeal matters should be applied. Finally,[478] he tries to explain that one may only obtain quasi-possession and quasi-ownership with regard to these incorporeal things.

503. As I have remarked above with regard to the sui generis right having to be developed with regard to the protection of databases – if too many examples of special cases or exceptions start occurring, it might be time to go back to the drawing board and revamp the entire system. Unfortunately, the first stopgap solution to the problem of immaterial goods, namely the law of intellectual property, has become so ingrained into the very warp and woof of international and national law, that such

472. (1985) Obiter (Law Journal of the University of Port Elizabeth), at 1.
473. Second ed. (1989), at 20.
474. 'Immaterial things' as opposed to the prior 'material things'.
475. C.G. van der Merwe, *Sakereg*, 2nd ed. (1989), 5 n.14, where he mentions usufruct and using personal rights as surety.
476. *Ibid.*, at 22.
477. *Ibid.*, at 25.
478. *Ibid.*, at 37.

a total rethink seems unlikely. More likely is a recurrence of 'special cases', sui generis protection and quasi-rights. The full implication of this might be a gradual lessening of importance of the law of things, with its material objects, in favour of an increasing emphasis on the law of intellectual property. The latter can at least claim the capacity to protect immaterial objects, including the most valuable asset of the twentieth century, namely information. Criminal law is likely to find application as isolated islands grafted onto intellectual property statutes to give them 'teeth', as is already the case in South Africa with the exception of the law of trade secrets.

504. To return to my above-mentioned article on the theft of information – I then tried to show that money has practically ceased to exist in corporeal form but that this 'incorporeal' could still be stolen in our present criminal law. A 'quick and dirty' solution to this would be for the criminal law to go its own way and simply define 'property' to also include intangibles, but this could lead to a dichotomy between criminal law and private law which might prove fatal to any coherent legal system.

505. Fortunately, this problem has attracted the attention of a private law academic in the shape of Duard Kleyn, then dean of the law faculty of the University of Pretoria. In an article entitled 'Dogmatiese probleme rakende die rol van onstoflike sake in die sakereg',[479] Kleyn also recommends that the concept of a thing ('saak') be extended to include incorporeals. He attributes the present clinging to the outdated concept of corporeal things to judicial conservatism and traditionalism even though in practice examples occur of real rights in incorporeal things. He does not want to go so far as to give the right holder to a patent the title of 'owner', however and suggests that he (or she) be seen as the holder of a limited real right. After exploring the traditional features of a thing, such as controllability, separateness, etc., he recommends the following new definition of a thing: 'Anything whether corporeal or incorporeal that is of use or value to man and which is regarded *in commercio*'.

506. Interestingly enough, this definition is so wide that it would quite probably include information too, with interesting implications for the law of intellectual property. If one could really buy and sell copyrighted computer programs, for instance, the whole licensing of use and (theoretical) return or destruction of presently licensed information would probably come to an end.

507. The question of the ownership of information has also exercised the mind of a South African specialist in the field of the law of intellectual property. In a groundbreaking article,[480] Esmè Duplessis argues that the right to information is actually an immaterial property right that has developed next to other similar rights, such as patent and copyright.

---

479. 'Dogmatical problems with regard to the role of immaterial things in the Law of Things', De Jure (Legal Journal of the University of Pretoria) (1993), at 1ff.
480. *Modern Business Law (MB)* (1985) 61 at 69.

508. This is, however, in conflict with the case of *Dun and Bradstreet v. SA Merchants Combined Credit Bureau (Cape) (Pty) Ltd* [481] where the basis of the action for trade secret was held to lie in competition law. Ms du Plessis' viewpoint appears to be rooted in the subjective rights school of legal theory, since she specifically mentions that confidential information has an independent existence from its bearer and that it has inherent economic value. In an article entitled 'Vruggebruik ten aansien van Ontginningsregte',[482] P.J. Badenhorst distinguishes between this 'subjective rights approach' and the 'traditional' approach[483] as far as the law of things is concerned, with regard to the proper classification of a usufruct in respect of mineral rights. He does not feel that it is necessary to widen the traditional definition of a thing to include incorporeal matter (as Kleyn did), since his own particular problem with a usufruct on a mineral right may also be solved by means of the subjective rights theory. In fact, he feels that the Kleyn definition might be so wide as to run the risk of vagueness. Nevertheless, Badenhorst's own approach simply puts forward a possible solution for rights on other rights and he does not venture a solution for rights in information.

509. This has been attempted by Tertius Geldenhuys, also building upon the foundation of subjective rights. In his doctoral thesis, entitled *Die Regsbeskerming van Inligting* [484] he explores the question as to whether information can ever be the subject of rights. By applying the subjective rights test for a legal object, he finds that certain categories of information, such as trade secret, do comply. The test is that the object:

(1) has to be of value to some or other legal subject and fulfil a need of that subject;
(2) has to be 'toedeelbaar' (apportionable) to a legal subject to the exclusion of other legal subjects – which means that something which is freely available such as air (and information in general) would not qualify;[485]
(3) if the apportionment serves a 'gemeenskapsordenende funksie' (orders society).[486]

510. The further development of the subjective rights approach to also encompass information[487] seems conceptually more promising than developing a number of quasi- and sui generis-rights in the law of things, but the question remains

481. 1968 (1) SA 209(C).
482. 'Usufruct in respect of Mineral Rights', P.J. Badenhorst, *Stellenbosch Law Review* 3 (1993): 394ff.
483. Of which Kleyn is considered to be an exponent.
484. Unisa LL.D. (1993).
485. This theory does not adequately reflect the commodity-like nature of information, which might be of value to a society. Cf. the so-called 'information gap' from which an entire continent such as Africa might be suffering.
486. In a quaint remark, which dates the subjective rights theory badly, Geldenhuys cites the subjective rights argument that possession of pornography can never be true law, since it does not 'order society'. This would mean that one could with impunity remove merchandise from a Hustler shop since it does not enjoy legal protection. These items might be morally repugnant but that does not mean that one can arbitrarily deprive them of their undoubted economic value.
487. Or at least, some kinds of information.

whether this solution would be acceptable internationally. In Germany, an argument has been made out for a right to 'Daten', which is described as *informationellen Rechtsgutes* [488] and which has developed as a result of new information techniques. In her work entitled *Der Strafrechtliche Schutz der Computerdaten gegen die Angriffsformen der Spionage, Sabotage und des Zeitdiebstahls*,[489] Ingeborg Schulze-Heiming argues that whereas the first industrial revolution replaced human muscle power by machines, the second industrial revolution[490] is replacing human *Geisteskraft* [491] by machines. As a result of the corresponding increase in the value of 'Computerdaten', possession of this has become a new right which is analogous to the older real rights. On the other hand, society needs a free flow of information and the author thus categorizes general information as 'ein freies (öffentliches) Gut ein Allgemeingut und wird nur ausnahmeweis in Form des Immaterialgüterschutzrechts individual-rechtlich zugeordnet'.[492] In dealing with the legal position of *Daten* the law will have to make use of the law of things, intellectual property rights as well as the *Geheimnissphäre* [493] which every individual (and legal person?) possesses. (The author's argument seems to boil down to the fact that the fields of private law and intellectual property law (including trade secrets) will have to cooperate creatively in order to deal with information.)

III. Conclusion

511. To sum up – the entire legal foundation for protecting information still seems to be built on concrete which has not set yet, and this will probably not change until we have more clarity on the precise nature of information. Certain representatives from the traditional approach as well as the subjective approach to the law of things seem willing to extend their definition of thing to also include incorporeals, but there is still some resistance to this from equally respected experts in the field. Authors such as Geldenhuys and Tony Twine have wildly disparate ideas of concepts like 'data', 'knowledge', and 'information'. For what it is worth, a personal[494] definition of information would run as follows: 'Information is defined as 'knowledge' (desired) items of knowledge, news'.

512. Read with the definition of 'knowledge' the definition of 'information' in the previous paragraph would again seem to be centred around a specific person's

488. (An) 'Informational Legal Thing'.
489. I. Schulze-Heiming, *The Protection by Criminal Law of Computer Data against the forms of attack of espionage sabotage and Theft of Time* (1995) at 1.
490. Which I would prefer calling the third wave, or 'the information revolution'.
491. Roughly translatable as 'mental power'.
492. I. Schulze-Heiming, *The Protection by Criminal Law of Computer Data against the forms of attack of espionage sabotage and Theft of Time* (1995) at 4. and freely translatable as: 'A free (public) good, a common good which only in exceptional cases is reducible to individual disposition by means of intellectual property law'.
493. Literally 'Sphere of secrecy'.
494. Term on loan from the Oxford Concise Dictionary.

spectrum of knowledge (range of information), but to go further than that by including desired items of knowledge. Information, therefore, implies a potential marketability, which will revert to below when the so-called commodification of information is dealt with. Marrying this to Schulze-Henning's views above, it seems that information should be a free-flowing commodity to which everyone should have a right (*Gemeingut*). When this has been transmuted into a private individual's range of knowledge, however, that knowledge deserves protection since it is a marketable good.

513. Unless the law of things starts dealing satisfactorily with the marketability side of incorporeals, and specifically with information as a commodity, it runs the risk of being overtaken by events. I have explored the value of information in an article entitled 'Knowledge is the key to riches – is the Law (or anything else) protecting it adequately?'[495] The article attempts to trace the dynamic development as information as a precious commodity which does not (nearly) attract the same type of protection which the law gives to other valuables such as land or precious metals.

§3. Computers and the Law of Delict

I. Introduction

514. As with the Law of Contract, the South African Law of Delict is based on Roman-Dutch law. According to most South African sources, a delict is defined as 'the wrongful and culpable act of a person which causes harm to another'.[496] Because these terms are very wide, it is obvious that the South African law is based more on general principle than the casuistic approach to 'tort law' in the US and the UK. In line with this general approach and with the Roman law, the South African Law of Delict distinguishes between 'harm' to one's pocket for which patrimonial damages may be claimed and 'harm' to one's personality rights for which *solatio* ('solace') might be obtained in the form of money.[497] For the former the *actio legis aquiliae* is available and for the latter the *actio iniuriarum*. Via the Roman-Dutch law, an action for pain and suffering of Germanic origin has also been introduced into South African law by which non-patrimonial damages for pain and suffering may be claimed.

II. The Elements of a Delict

515. In terms of the above definition, five delictual elements may be distinguished. These are:

495. PER (Potchefstroom Elektroniese Regstydskrif) 2008 4 at 1.
496. *See* Alheit, *Issues of Liability Arising from the Use of Expert Systems* (1997) (unpublished LL.D. thesis 1997 Pretoria, University of South Africa) at 140.
497. Alheit speaks of 'satisfaction or sentimental damages', *Ibid.*, at 141.

(a) voluntary conduct.
(b) wrongfulness.
(c) fault.
(d) causation;
(e) damage.

516. Each of these will now be examined with a view to their applicability to computer law.

A. *Conduct*

517. This element has to consist of a voluntary human act or omission. A juristic person such as a company, a closed corporation or a software house may commit a delict through the conduct of one of its human members. An omission to take reasonable steps to ensure that sold hardware or software is compliant with statutory standards may lead to patrimonial damages being claimable by means of the *actio legis aquiliae*. The *actio iniuriarum* on the other hand would come into play where a person's right to privacy has been infringed by her employer reading her e-mail, for example, or where her feelings have been hurt in a 'flame war' in a discussion group.

B. *Wrongfulness*

518. This element of a delict might be seen as a very subjective test, so that both wrongdoer and victim might each feel herself to be on the side of the angels in that she acted 'reasonably'. The courts, therefore, work with a general criterion of reasonableness, namely the *boni mores*,[498] also referred to as the legal convictions of the community.

519. According to Alheit,[499] however, the test is an objective ex post facto[500] process, said to be viewed by the courts from the perspective of the 'reasonable bystander'. The South African Constitution, and in particular the Bill of Rights, is also a factor to be taken into account in deciding whether particular conduct had been wrongful.

520. An important factor in testing for wrongfulness in a particular instance is to determine whether a ground of justification existed. There is no *numerus clausus* of these grounds but typical examples might be self-defence, necessity, consent, or authorization. In the latter case, the power of the state to authorize certain action

498. Literally the 'good customs' (of a community).
499. K. Alheit, *Issues of Liability Arising from the Use of Expert Systems* (1997) (unpublished LL.D. thesis 1997 Pretoria, University of South Africa) at 149.
500. Literally 'from after the fact' – judging or acting on something after it has already happened.

would have to be tested against the protection that the Constitution provides to certain human rights. A typical example might be a request by the police to monitor the e-mail of a suspected criminal that would have to be weighed against his right to privacy that is guaranteed by the Constitution. This guarantee is not absolute, however, and might have to be limited if it is found by the court to be absolutely necessary in terms of the limitations clause.[501] (It is exactly this type of scenario that makes governments less enthusiastic about powerful encryption software in the hands of its subjects, as might be seen from the recent fall-out between Apple and the FBI. The latter wanted the former to provide a 'backdoor' into its machines, which the computer company declined to do because of privacy considerations.)

521. According to Alheit,[502] wrongfulness might arise both from the infringement of a subjective right[503] or from the breach of a legal duty. The latter would occur in the case of liability for an omission or in the causing of pure economic loss. The *boni mores* test would again have to be applied in borderline cases. She warns that this legal duty (sometimes referred to as a 'duty of care') forms part of the element of wrongfulness and that it should not be confused with the test for negligence that is part of fault, the next element. The 'duty of care' doctrine with regard to negligence is an English doctrine used with reference to their specific tort of negligence and 'should be avoided as it causes confusion between the test for wrongfulness and the test for negligence'.

C. Fault

522. This might take the form of either intention or negligence. Real-life examples are mostly due to the latter, particularly due to adequate standards not being adhered to. An exception might be deliberate sabotage by means of unlawful access to a computer system, for instance by spreading a lawful virus on the victim's network. This matter will be more fully dealt with in the chapter on computer crime.

523. The test for negligence is taken from *Kruger v. Coetzee* [504] and is as follows:

> For the purposes of liability culpa arises if –
>
> (a) a diligens paterfamilias [505] in the position of the defendant –
>
> (i) would foresee the reasonable possibility of his conduct injuring another in his person or property and causing him patrimonial loss; and

501. Section 36 of Act 108 of 1996 (the Constitution of South Africa).
502. K. Alheit, *Issues of Liability Arising from the Use of Expert Systems* (1997) (unpublished LL. D. Thesis 1997 Pretoria, University of South Africa) at 153.
503. This has been dealt with above under the law of things.
504. 1966 (2) SA 428 (A).
505. A diligent (male) head of the family who is presumed to be pretty responsible.

(ii) would take reasonable steps to guard against such occurrence; and
(b) the defendant failed to take such steps.

524. This *diligens paterfamilias* (or *materfamilias*, I suppose) is supposed to be the reasonable man, the 'man on the Clapham omnibus', who is neither exceptionally bright or cautious, nor dull-witted or reckless.[506] This test could turn out to be difficult to apply as far as computers are concerned. Is the reasonable man/woman computer literate? If so, what does this standard actually mean?

525. Alheit again deals separately with professional negligence by professionals from whom one might have expected a higher standard of care. According to the maxim *imperitia culpae adnumeratur* [507] persons who undertake activities that require skill without such possessing such skill will be held to be negligent at best, perhaps even as fraudulent. Contributory negligence on the part of the claimant might however lessen the quantum (amount) of the claim. Michalson warns that loss of commercial data is likely to be much more expensive in damages than loss of domestic data.[508]

D. Causation

526. In this case, one has to distinguish between factual and legal causation. Factual causation is tested according to the *conditio sine qua non*[509] test. This means that 'but for' the causing factor the present result would not have occurred. Put negatively – if one thinks away the factor of causation, the present result should also fall away. This might, of course, lead back to Adam and Eve causation, or to the primeval slime (depending on one's worldview) so some limiting factor has to be found. This is where legal causation comes in. In the past, the theories of adequate causation, of direct consequences, of fault and of reasonable foreseeability have all had their day, but in *S v. Mokgethi* [510] the Appellate Division has opted for a 'flexible approach', meaning that no single criterion for legal causation can be applied to all factual situations.

527. The situation with regard to software is not clear. An argument that the creators of chips that are later embedded in other products might be too remote in their causal connection with the end user to be seen as having caused the unfortunate result.

506. K. Alheit, *Issues of Liability Arising from the Use of Expert Systems* (1997) (unpublished LL. D. thesis 1997 Pretoria, University of South Africa) 156.
507. Lack of skill is taken as negligence.
508. *South Africa & The Millennium Time Bomb: A Guide to the Legal Issues* (1998) at 54.
509. Literally the 'condition without which not'.
510. 1990 (1) SA 32 (A).

E. Loss

528. Alheit[511] states that the damage caused by a delict is seen broadly as encompassing both patrimonial and non-patrimonial loss. Both are compensated for by money in the form of 'damages' awarded by the court. Pure economic loss refers to patrimonial loss not caused by injury to the plaintiff's person or property

F. A Typical Cyber-Delict: Defamation on the Internet

529. The spectre of online delictual ability raises the interesting possibility of defamation on the Internet. This topic has been explored locally in an article entitled 'Defamation on the Internet and other computer networks.[512] After some comparative law, the author also examined the South African situation, which differs appreciably because of the Roman-Dutch law still being in full flower locally. The definition of defamation in South African law is as follows: 'The wrongful intentional publication of words or behaviour concerning another which has the tendency to undermine his status, good name or reputation.'[513]

530. In her article, Nel remarks on the fact that even though there is no doubt that the person uttering such remarks on a public medium such as the Internet has complied with the above requirements, there is some doubt about a person who repeats, confirms, or directs attention to these remarks. She suggests that the liability of online service providers who exercise no editorial control over the messages on their bulletin boards should be compared to that of distributors or vendors (such as news agencies or bookshops) whose liability is based on negligence.[514] The typical Internet bugbear of jurisdiction again raises its head but Nel shows that according to South African law, the plaintiff has the choice of either instituting action in the jurisdiction where the cause of action arose[515] or in the defendant's jurisdictional court. If the defendant remains physically absent, action will most likely have to be instituted in her home country, following that country's laws.

531. Unfortunately, Nel does not write a lot about the major defences to a defamation claim, namely truth and public benefit, fair comment, and qualified privilege. One would think that these defences should go a long way on a medium that is known to be free and unregulated.

---

511. K. Alheit, *Issues of Liability Arising from the Use of Expert Systems* (1997) (unpublished LL. D. thesis 1997 Pretoria, University of South Africa) at 167.
512. By Sanette Nel in XXX CILSA (1997) at 154ff. For an update by the same author see Chapter 10 on 'Freedom of Expression' in *ICT Law* by Van der Merwe et al., at 531ff.
513. *Neethling's Law of Personality* (1996) by Neethling, Potgieter & Visser at 140.
514. XXX CILSA (1997) at 168-169.
515. Would that be where the server is physically located, or the computer on which the words were first typed?

III. The Liability of Internet Service Providers (ISPs)

532. ISPs[516] form an important part of the Internet backbone in South Africa. They have organized themselves into an autonomous body called ISPA (Internet Service Providers of South Africa), and this body has often taken strong positions regarding matters which it sees as vital to the continued success of Internet-related matters in South Africa. This, of course, includes the possible legal liability of ISPs that they might incur while carrying out their responsibilities. As has been mentioned above, the ECT Act[517] has endeavoured to lighten the load of ISP by inserting a whole chapter entitled 'Limitation of Liability of Service Providers'.[518] A 'service provider' is defined[519] as 'any person providing information system services'.[520]

533. Section 73 of the ECT Act[521] exempts a service provider from liability for 'providing access to, or for operating facilities for information systems[522] or transmitting, routing, or storage of data messages via an information system under its control', provided that the service provider complies with four conditions. These four conditions require the service provider to play a largely passive role and to act as a mere conduit with regard to the transmission of data by means of the information system. Even if he (or she) merely performs such a passive 'post office' role, a competent court may still order a service provider to terminate or prevent unlawful activity in terms of any other law.[523]

534. Section 74 exempts service providers from liability for caching data provided that this temporary storage is simply for the purposes of making the transmission service more effective. A number of conditions again apply, which are mostly based on the fact that the service provider does not interfere with the data in any way and (interestingly) 'does not interfere with the lawful use of technology, widely recognized and used by industry, to obtain information on the use of the data'.[524] This probably relates to the statistical monitoring of the movement of data between websites. The same qualification stated with regard to the previous section, namely that a competent court may still order a service provider to terminate or prevent unlawful activity in terms of any other law, again applies.[525]

---

516. Which phrase will include network operators for present purposes?
517. Act 25 of 2002.
518. Chapter XI, containing ss 70–79.
519. By s.70 of the Act.
520. 'Information systems services' are in turn defined by s. 1 of the ECT Act as 'the provision of connections, the operation of facilities for information systems, the provision of access to information systems, the transmission or routing of data messages between or among points specified by a user and the processing and storage of data, at the individual request of the recipient of the service'.
521. Act 25 of 2002.
522. 'Information systems' are defined by s. 1 of the ECT Act as: 'a system for generating, sending, receiving, storing, displaying or otherwise processing data messages and includes the Internet'.
523. Section 73(3).
524. Section 74(1)(d).
525. Section 74(2).

535. Section 75 contains similar provisions for protecting service providers with regard to hosting activities. Again, this exemption depends on the service provider playing a mainly passive role with regard to the actual data itself, but contains a new twist:

> The limitations on liability established by this section do not apply to a service provider unless it has designated an agent to receive notifications of infringement and has provided through its services, including on its web sites in locations accessible to the public, the name, address, phone number and e-mail address of the agent.[526]

536. Despite the considerable protection that this clause presents to service providers, I have personally not seen many notices regarding the above-mentioned agents appearing on South African websites. The same qualification stated with regard to the previous section, namely that a competent court may still order a service provider to terminate or prevent unlawful activity in terms of any other law, again applies.[527] In order not to allow any internal delegation to escape liability, another subsection excludes the application of the present section if the recipient of the service is acting under the authority or control of the service provider.[528]

537. Two other provisions in the chapter under discussion may also prove to be very useful to service providers. Firstly, a service provider will not be held liable for providing links to offending sites by means of information location tools (such as hyperlinks), provided that he (or she) has again played the passive role described with regard to the corresponding paragraphs immediately above.[529] Furthermore, there is no general obligation on service providers to 'monitor the data which it transmits or stores',[530] or to 'actively seek facts and circumstances indicating an unlawful activity'.[531]

526. Section 75(2).
527. Section 75(3).
528. Section 75(4).
529. Section 76 of the ECT Act 25 of 2002.
530. Section 78(1)(a).
531. Section 78(1)(b).

Part VIII. The Protection of Privacy

Chapter 1. Some Thoughts on Privacy in a Digital World

§1. Introduction

538. At this point, foreign readers should have some idea of the South African law of delict.[532] The example of defamation dealt with above is a typical example of a personality right being infringed and then compensated for by means of the modern version of the old Roman actio iniuriarum. In terms of the Roman-Dutch common law, privacy can be dealt with in the same way – our main problem now is the rapidly changing situation of privacy in a world that has shrunk to the size of a global village.[533] The shop-worn words of Marshall McLuhan in respect of the 'global village' have become truer than perhaps even he could see: 'As electrically contracted, the globe is no more than a village.''[534]

539. Note that the term 'contract' as used in the previous paragraph should not be read in its legal sense, but more in the sense of having been electronically shrunk.

540. In June 1998, the Federal Trade Commission of the US released its long-awaited report on Internet privacy. It recommended that legislation be passed barring websites from collecting personal data from young children but leaving the situation with regard to adults open. After about three years of studying more than 1,400 websites targeted at consumers, the agency found that while 85% of the sites collect personal data from users, only 14% of those rates tell users what is happening. Only 2% of all sites provide a comprehensive privacy policy giving users details on how they will use the data. According to the then FTC chairman Robert Pitofsky, 'Concerns about personal privacy are repeatedly cited as the most important reason not to get on the Internet.'[535]

532. *See* **Part VII, Ch. 2,** §3, paras 514–531.
533. *See* in general Chapter 9 on Data Privacy Law in *ICT Law* (2022) by Van der Merwe et al., 387ff. This specific section was written by Prof. A Roos, an expert on privacy law.
534. *Understanding Media* (1964) at 12. McLuhan is also the originator of the popular phrase 'The medium is the message'.
535. *Source*: ZDNet of 4 Jun. 1998.

541. There might be good reason for leaving the situation with regard to adults open. In his work, *Law in a Digital World,*[536] Ethan Katsch points out that the individual whose privacy is at stake is no longer simply a victim, but a collaborator. 'Personal information is no longer obtained surreptitiously or illegally but is given away or sold.' The old nomenclature of 'one's home is one's castle' and 'zones of privacy' has a strong territorial connotation, according to Katsch. If this is so, it sounds like a throwback to the First Wave,[537] with its agricultural revolution, in which land was the currency of power and standing. According to Katsch, the new concept of privacy should perhaps rather be of 'a condition that allows the individual freedom to choose when to establish a relationship and when not'. According to this test, it seems obvious that the surreptitious collection of personal data described in the previous paragraph should not be allowed, because it leaves the individual no choice with regard to his or her personality rights.

§2. Privacy in South Africa

542. In South Africa, in addition to protection by the Roman-Dutch common law, the right to privacy is protected by section 14 of the Constitution.[538] With constitutions working mostly vertically, this protection is aimed mainly against the state. After a long gestation period, legislation has been passed by the South African legislature to give concrete effect to this constitutional right, but now also to provide protection against the prying eyes of your fellow citizens! The Protection of Personal Information (POPI) Act[539] followed upon a Discussion Paper from the Law Commission and from a draft bill on the protection of personal information. An 'Information Regulator'[540] was established at the end of 2016 and regulations were drafted in 2018. The act is in force as from 1 July 2020 with a period of grace for implementation of one year. As from 1 July 2021, therefore, numerous websites have posted notices informing users of their right to privacy and containing requests from the owner of the site to its visitors to use their personal data. This requirement applies to both public and private sector websites.

536. (1995) at 231.
537. *See* Alvin Toffler *The Third Wave* (1980) whose catchy metaphor has been used before in the present work.
538. Act 108 of 1996.
539. Act 4 of 2013. See *ICT Law* (2022) by Van der Merwe et al., at 476ff.
540. The Information Regulator is tasked with oversight over both the POPI and the PAI Acts. The latter acronym (PAIA) deals with the Protection of Access to Information Act, 2 of 2000.

Chapter 2. Analysing POPI: The Protection of Personal Information

§1. Guidelines to the Act

543. Several guidelines have been laid down by POPI for the processing of personal information. In the first place the condition of accountability has been laid down as a prerequisite to such processing. A second principle specifies limits to processing based on principles such as the lawfulness of such processing, minimality in processing and grounds of justification for such processing. In the third place, specification of the purpose for collecting the data should be made quite clear. There should be limitation on any further processing, once the main goal for collecting the data has been accomplished. Practical steps should be taken to guarantee information quality. Openness and transparency between parties is also an important principle in collecting the data. Security safeguards should be put in place in order to guarantee the quality of the data collected and also to guard against unauthorized or unlawful access to such data. Data subject participation forms the last, but by no means the least, of these POPI privacy guidelines.

§2. Case Law on the Act

544. In one of the few decided cases on privacy in South Africa, it was argued in *Mistry v. Interim Medical and Dental Council of South Africa*,[541] that the passing on of personal information from one medicine control inspector to another might be an invasion of the constitutional right to privacy.

§3. Definitions Contained in the Act

545. The new statutory definition of 'processing' is very wide and runs as follows:

> any operation or activity or any set of operations, whether or not by automatic means, concerning personal information and including
>
> (a) the collection, receipt, recording, organization, collation, storage, updating or modification, retrieval, alteration, consultation, or use, dissemination by means of transmission, distribution or making available in any form, merging linking, as well as blocking, erasure or destruction of information;
> (b) dissemination by means of transmission, distribution or making available in any other form;
> (c) merging, linking, as well as restriction, degradation, erasure or destruction of information.

541. 1998 (4) SA 1127 (CC) 1145.

546. It has been argued that 'the above definition is so wide that one can argue that processing could be seen as any action performed on personal information'.[542]

547. The act then also defines 'personal information' as 'information relating to an identifiable being, natural person and, where it is applicable, an identifiable, existing juristic person'.

548. In turn, a 'responsible party' is defined as 'the public or private body or any other person which, alone, or in conjunction with others, determines the purpose of and means for processing personal information'.[543]

§4. Enforcement of the POPI Act

549. It is interesting to note that, differing from many other South African statutes, POPI does not revert to the Criminal Courts to enforce its provisions. It creates a quasi-judicial 'Regulator' to whom parties may resort in order to enforce the provisions of the act.[544] Having investigated a complaint, the Regulator may decide to refer the matter to an Enforcement Committee which may make recommendations in this regard. In suitable cases the Regulator may then serve the transgressor with an enforcement notice directing the party concerned to stop processing information, to take certain steps, or to refrain from taking certain steps.

550. Only in extreme cases may resort be taken to the Criminal Law in order to bring non-co-operative customers to a final reckoning.[545]

§5. The Impact of South African Legislation (Other than POPI) on Privacy

551. In other legislative activity in the area of privacy, the Interception and Monitoring Prohibition Act[546] has now been replaced by the Regulation of Interception of Communications and Provision of Communication-Related Information Act,[547] and certain of its provisions have aroused a degree of controversy. It may be of interest to note that the concept of 'interception' in terms of the latest act may be wide enough to include the monitoring of the use of a website by a customer or employee. This would have severe privacy implications.

542. By A Roos in *ICT Law* (2022) by Van der Merwe et al., at 478.
543. *Supra* at 483.
544. *Supra* at 522ff.
545. See *ICT Law* (2022) by Van der Merwe et al., at 528ff.
546. Act 127 of 1992.
547. Act 70 of 2002.

552. Although the new act stems from a predecessor that basically prohibited interception and monitoring activities[548] the later act permits interception under a variety of circumstances.

553. The ECT Act[549] does include a voluntary regime for the protection of personal information particularly. There does not seem to be much reward in adhering to these guidelines, however, save if one could perhaps affix a plaque, or rosette, to the bottom of one's website, boasting 'voluntary compliance with the privacy provisions of the ECT Act'.

554. When the ECT was being drafted, it was felt that a compulsory procedure should be prescribed for collecting private and personal information obtained by means of electronic transactions. This procedure would also seem to be a good idea in the light of the protection of privacy as set out in section 14 of the Constitution.[550]

555. Nevertheless, pressure was exerted from the government to keep these principles in the Act as a voluntary regime. Users could then choose to subscribe to them and then use their compliance as a marketing tool. These principles were set out in section 51 in the ECT Act and turn on factors such as the consent of the data subject, disclosure to the subject of the purpose for which the information was being collected and keeping to that purpose.

556. The data controller (the collector of the personal data) should also keep a record of the personal information and the reason why it being collected and may not disclose any such information, unless compelled to do so by court order or authorized by the data subject. The controller should also keep a record of the third parties to whom the information has been disclosed and destroy all personal information which has become obsolete.

557. One of the most interesting clauses is section 51(9), which determines the following with regard to statistical information:

> A party controlling personal information may use that personal information to compile profiles for statistical purposes and may freely trade with such profiles and statistical data, as long as the profiles or statistical data cannot be linked to any specific subject by a third party.

558. This clause tends to illustrate the difference between anonymous 'data' and 'information' that may be linked by someone to a specific individual. Data may still have considerable commercial value but does not threaten any constitutional rights of privacy. For this reason, it need not be protected by the Constitution or the resultant legislation.

548. As the title of the Act indicates.
549. Act 25 of 2002.
550. Act 108 of 1996.

Selected Bibliography

Books (Including Chapters) and Treatises

Alheit, K. *Issues of Liability Arising from the Use of Expert Systems* (unpublished LL.D. thesis, 1997, Pretoria, University of South Africa).

Bothma, Botha J.C. & P. Geldenhuys et al., *Managing E-Commerce* (Cape Town: Juta, 2004).

Buys, R. (ed.). *Cyberlaw@SA* (Pretoria: Van Schaik, (2000).

Buys, R. (ed.). *Cyberlaw@SA* (Pretoria: Van Schaik, (2004).

Carstens, J. & P. Lucouw et al., *E-Commerce in Practice* (Vanderbijlpark: Coral Publishers, 2004).

Forsyth C *Private International Law* (Wolters Kluwer 2014).

Geldenhuys T. *Regsbeskerming van Inligting* (unpublished LL.D. thesis, 1993, Pretoria, University of South Africa).

Hofman, J. *Cyberlaw* (Cape Town: Ampersand Press, 1999).

Kiat, T.S. *Legal Aspects of Doing Business in Singapore* (Addison Wesley 1996).

Katsch, E. *Law in a Digital World* (Oxford: Oxford University Press, 1995).

Maré, E. *Evaluering van kontraktipes by die verskaffing van rekenaarprogrammatuur* (*Evaluating types of contract for the supply of computer programmes*) unpublished LL.M. thesis, 1995, Potchefstroom, PUCHE).

Merges, Menell, Lemley & Jorde, *Intellectual Property in the New Technological Age* (Aspen, 1997) at 523.

Ndlovu, P. N. *Competition Law in South Afric*a (Kluwer Law 2018).

Schoeman, E. et al *Private International Law* (Wolters Kluwer 2014).

Silberberg & Schoeman, *Law of Property* (Durban: Butterworths, 1992).

Snail & Papadopoulos Cyberlaw@SA III (Pretoria: Van Schaik, 2012).

Strunz, B. *The Interface of Competition Law, Industrial Policy, and Development: The Case of South Africa* (Munich Studies on Innovation and Competition, Vol 8, 2018).

Van der Merwe, C.G. *Sakereg*, (Cape Town: Juta, 1989).

Van der Merwe, D.P. *Computers and the Law* (Cape Town: Juta, 1986).

Van der Merwe, D.P. *Computers and the Law* (Cape Town: Juta, 2000).

Van der Merwe, D.P. et al., *ICT Law* (Durban: LexisNexis, 2008).

Van der Merwe, D.P. et al., *ICT Law* (Durban: LexisNexis, 2016).

Van der Merwe, D.P. et al., *ICT Law* (Durban: LexisNexis, 2022)

Selected Bibliography

Articles

'A Common Law Perspective on Computer-Related Crimes', *THRHR* (2004): 193 and 375.

'A Few Remarks and Questions Concerning the New Constitution', *THRHR*, (1997): 377 at 386 n28.

'An Evaluation of Selected Aspects of the Alternative Dispute Resolution', *SA Merc LJ* (2007): 165–185.

'Choice of Law in Internet Copyright Disputes', *SA Mercantile Law Journal* (1999): 268.

'Computer Crime': *Obiter* (1983): 124ff.

'Computers and Crime', *SACC* (1984): 262.

'Diefstal van Onliggaamlike Sake met Spesifieke Verwysing na Rekenaars' ('Theft of Intangibles with specific reference to Computers)', *SACC* (1985): 29.

'Dispute Resolution in Cyberspace', *SA Merc LJ* (2000): 199–208

'Dogmatiese Probleme rakende die rol van onstoflike sake in die sakereg' ('Dogmatic Problems in connection with immaterial goods in the Law of Things'), De Jure (1993): 1.

'Enkele Gedagtes aangaande Mobiele Handeldryf of M-Handel ('M-Commerce')', ('Some Thoughts regarding Mobile Trading or M-Commerce'), *THRHR* 69 (2006): 318.

'Information Technology Crime: A New Paradigm Is Needed', *THRHR* (2007): 309ff.

'Protection of Computer Programs by Copyright in South Africa', *Stellenbosch Law Review* 1(1995): 89.

'Teorie van Subjektiewe Regte', ('A Theory of Subjective Rights') *THRHR* 21 (1958): 12 and 98.

'The real meaning of Apple's battle with the FBI over encryption', *TIME* magazine of 7/3/2016 18–19.

'Vruggebruik ten aansien van Ontginningsregte', ('Usufruct in connection with Mining Rights'), *Stellenbosch Law Review* (1993): 349.

'XBRL and the Law: Implications of Markup Languages', (2011) *Journal of Contemporary Roman-Dutch Law (JCR-DL)* 418ff

Case Law

Campbell v. Hall, (1774) 1 Cowper 204, 98 ER 1045.

Dun and Bradstreet v. SA Merchants Combined Credit Bureau (Cape) Pty Ltd, (1968) SA 209 (C).

Fax Directories (Pty) Ltd v. SA Fax Listings CC, (1990) (2) SALR 164 (D).

Galago Publishers (Pty) Ltd and Another v. Erasmus, (1989) (1) SALR 276 (A).

Meter Patent Development (Pty) Ltd v. Ash Electronic Industries & Another, (1995) Burrell's Patent Law Reports 185.

Metro Polis T/A Transactive (Pty) Ltd v. Naidoo T/A African Products, 759 *JOC* (T).

Mistry v. Interim Medical and Dental Council of South Africa 1998 (4) SA 1127 (CC).

Narlis v. South African Bank of Athens, (1976) (2) SA 573 (A).

Ndlovu v. Minister of Correctional Services and Another, (2006) 4 All SA 165 (W).

Northern Office Micro Computers (Pty Ltd) and Others v. Rosenstein, (1981) (4) SALR 123 (C).
Pastel Software v. Pink Software (Pty) Ltd, 399 JOC (T).
S v. Baleka (1), (1986) (4) SA 192 (T).
S v. Mpumlo, (1986) (3) SA 485 (E).
S v. Ndiki, (2007) 2 All SA 185 (Ck).
S v. Ramgobin, (1986) (4) SA (N).
S v. Singh, (1975) (1) SA 330 (N).
S v. Van der Berg, (1991) (1) SACR 104 (T).
Tolima (Pty) Ltd v. Cugacius Motor Accessories (Pty) Ltd, (1983) (3) SALR 504 (E).

Selected Bibliography

Index

The numbers here refer to paragraph numbers.

Index

Index

Ingram Content Group UK Ltd.
Milton Keynes UK
UKHW022007030523
421159UK00006B/231

9 789403 522869